HOW TO USE CHATGPT FOR AUTHORS: FROM IDEA TO PUBLISHED BOOK

HOW TO USE CHATGPT FOR AUTHORS:
FROM IDEA TO PUBLISHED BOOK
Copyright © 2025 by Dr. Constance Santego.

Copy Editor and Interior Design: Constance Santego
Book Layout: ©2017 BookDesignTemplates.com
Cover Design: Jennifer Louie

Ordering Information:
Quantity sales. Special discounts are available on quantity purchases by corporations, associations, and others. For details, contact the address below.

Trade paperback ISBN: 978-1-990062-69-8
eBook ISBN: 978-1-990062-70-4

Created and published In Canada. Printed and bound in the United States of America
First Edition
Published by Maximillian Enterprises
Kelowna, BC Canada
www.constancesantego.ca

Dedication

To the authors who still believe in magic—
not just the magic of storytelling,
but the magic of asking the right question
at exactly the right time.

May this book be a guide,
a spark,
and a trusted companion
as you transform your thoughts into legacy
and co-create with intelligence,
both within and beyond.

— Constance

HOW TO USE CHATGPT FOR AUTHORS: FROM IDEA TO PUBLISHED BOOK

Dr. Constance Santego

Maximillian Enterprises
Kelowna, BC

The Alchemy of Thought & Technology

Sacred Fusion for the Modern Author

This book is a bridge.
A meeting point where ancient storytelling meets modern intelligence.
Where intuition meets logic.
Where the whisper of the soul is amplified through code.

- It is for the **visionary author**, ready to create beyond the blank page.
- It is for the **storyteller**, who seeks clarity, momentum, and inspiration on demand.
- It is for the **teacher and guide**, crafting messages that matter.
- It is for the **creator**, shaping worlds, healing hearts, or awakening minds.

Within these pages, you'll learn how to turn your spark of an idea into a structured, soul-aligned book — not by surrendering your voice, but by deepening your process.

This is not a shortcut.
It is a **collaboration**.
A sacred toolset for authors who dare to co-create with intelligence — artificial and divine.

Crafted in alignment,
Dr. Constance Santego

ALSO BY DR. CONSTANCE SANTEGO

NOVELS

Illegitimate Grace

Okanagan Trilogy:

Beneath the Vineyards
Under the Okanagan Sun
Guardian of the Lake

The Nine Spiritual Gifts Series:
Journey of a Soul – (Vol 1 Michael)
Language of a Soul – (Vol 2 Gabriel)
Prophecy of a Soul – (Vol 3 Bath Kol)
Healing of a Soul – (Vol 4 Raphael)
Miracles of a Soul – (Vol 5 Hamied)
Knowledge of a Soul – (Vol 6 Raziel)
Wisdom of a Soul – (Vol 7 Uriel)
Faith of a Soul – (Vol 8 Pistis Sophia)

NONFICTION
The Intuitive Life, The Gift Of Prophecy, Third Edition
Fairy Tales, Dreams And Reality… Where Are You On Your
Path? Second Edition
Your Persona… The Mask You Wear
Archangel Michael's Soul Retrieval Guide
Tesla And The Future Of Energy Medicine
Beyond Tesla: *Advancing The Science Of Energy Healing*
Tesla's Code: *Mastering Energy, Frequency, And Creative Power*
Scaling Beyond 6 Figures: *Strategies for Health & Wellness
Professionals*
Beyond the Mind: *Harnessing the Power of Astral Projection for Creative
Awakening*
Bend, Don't Break: *Finding Your Way Back to Abundance*
Ring Therapy: *A Guide to Healing and Balance*
Ring Therapy Pocket Guide

Floraopathy™: *The Art and Science of Vibrational Healing with Essential Oils*

REIKI WISDOM, SERIES:

Angelic Lifestyle, a Vibrant Lifestyle
Angelic Lifestyle 42-Day Energy Cleanse
Reiki and the Power of The Joint Points: *Unlocking Energy Pathways for Healing* (Vol I)
Reiki and Karmic Healing: *Releasing Patterns From Past Lives* (Vol II)
Reiki and the Five Elements (Vol III)

SECRETS OF A HEALER, SERIES:
Magic Of Aromatherapy (Vol I)
Magic Of Reflexology (Vol II)
Magic Of The Gifts (Vol III)
Magic Of Muscle Testing (Vol IV)
Magic Of Iridology (Vol V)
Magic Of Massage (Vol VI)
Magic Of Hypnotherapy (Vol VII)
Magic Of Reiki (Vol VIII)
Magic Of Advanced Aromatherapy (Vol IX)
Magic Of Esthetics (Vol X)
The Reiki Master's Manual (Vol XI)

ADULT COLORING JOURNALS

SERIES-ZEN COLORING:
Quantum Energy and Mindful Living Journal (Vol 1)
Reiki Energy Journal (Vol 2)
Nine Spiritual Gifts Journal (Vol 3)
I Forgive Journal (Vol 4)

FOR CHILDREN
I am Big Tonight. I Don't Need the Light

Contents

"The power of authorship lies not in what we write alone, but in how boldly we ask the questions that bring the story to life."
—Dr. Constance Santego

Preface

When I first began writing, everything came from long nights, handwritten notes, stacks of research, and a quiet conversation between me and the page. The process was sacred — and still is — but like every evolving artist, I've learned that sacred doesn't mean stagnant.

Then came AI.
And with it, a flood of questions.

Would it replace creativity?
Would it cheapen originality?
Or… could it enhance the process, sharpen the message, and empower more voices to rise?

This book is my answer.

How to Use ChatGPT for Authors is not a technical manual — it's a companion. It is a guide for the modern author navigating new territory. A place where storytelling meets technology, where prompts become portals, and where the sacred act of writing is honored, not diminished, by innovation.

Here, you won't lose your voice.
You'll find new ways to use it.

Whether you write fiction, nonfiction, children's books, or memoirs… whether you're staring down your first blank page or refining your final chapter… this book will show you how to collaborate with AI ethically, effectively, and creatively.

This is for the author who still leads with intuition — but isn't afraid to use every tool available to make the message shine.

Welcome to the fusion of insight and innovation.
Welcome to the future of authorship.

Dr. Constance Santego

Note to Reader

This book was written for *you* — the dreamer with a message, the visionary with a story, the writer who knows there's something more inside waiting to come out.

If you've ever felt overwhelmed by the writing process…
If you've stared at a blinking cursor and wondered where to begin…
If you've wanted a writing partner that could keep pace with your ideas, help organize your thoughts, or simply cheer you on when inspiration runs dry —
Then you're exactly where you need to be.

This isn't about giving away your creativity.
It's about expanding it.

Throughout this book, you'll learn how to use ChatGPT as your assistant, co-creator, brainstorming partner, editor, and even marketer — while staying true to *your* voice, *your* values, and *your* vision.

Every tool you need is already within you.
This guide simply helps you activate it — faster, clearer, and with more joy.

Here's to your next book —
and the powerful new way you're about to write it.

— Constance

Learning Outcome

By the end of this book, you will be able to:

- **Confidently collaborate with ChatGPT** as a writing partner, using strategic prompts to enhance your creativity, productivity, and clarity.
- **Develop and structure your book** — whether fiction, nonfiction, or children's — with the help of AI-generated outlines, chapter ideas, and content flow.
- **Write compelling content faster**, including scenes, descriptions, teaching points, and emotional arcs, while maintaining your authentic voice.
- **Edit, refine, and rewrite** with ChatGPT's assistance to improve tone, pacing, grammar, and structure.
- **Create essential book components**, such as your back cover blurb, author bio, dedication, chapter titles, and metadata using targeted prompts.
- **Understand the legal, ethical, and creative considerations** of using AI in your writing practice.
- **Design marketing and publishing content** such as email campaigns, launch strategies, and keyword-rich descriptions.
- **Overcome writer's block, imposter syndrome, and tech overwhelm** with intuitive tools that support your unique workflow and goals.

This book is your complete guide to blending intuition with innovation, turning your ideas into impactful books — with ease, integrity, and inspiration.

Getting Started with ChatGPT

Free vs. Paid, What You Need, and Why It Matters

Before you can use ChatGPT to write, organize, or refine your book, you need to **access the tool itself.** Thankfully, it's easy — but there are some key differences between the free and paid versions you should know.

What Is ChatGPT and Where Do I Get It?

ChatGPT is an AI writing assistant developed by OpenAI. It's available online, on mobile apps, and can be used right from your browser.

Visit: chat.openai.com
Or download the **ChatGPT app** from the Apple App Store or Google Play.

To use it, you'll need to **create a free account** with your email address.

The Free Version (GPT-3.5)

- Includes **basic access** to ChatGPT's core features
- Runs on **GPT-3.5**, which is still powerful, but more limited
- Slower, less nuanced responses
- May not understand complex instructions or layered prompts as well

- Can't access tools like charts, image generation, or file uploads

Great for: Beginners, light writing help, brainstorming, quick drafting

Limitations for Authors:

- Can be repetitive or vague
- Doesn't always follow detailed structure requests
- Lacks deeper understanding of tone, pacing, or genre conventions

The Paid Version (ChatGPT Plus / GPT-4)

As of now, **ChatGPT Plus** costs **$20/month USD** and gives you access to **GPT-4-turbo**, the most advanced version.

This version:

- Responds with **more accuracy and creativity**
- Handles **complex, multi-step instructions** with ease
- Maintains **style and tone** more consistently
- Has access to **file uploads, image input, and plug-ins** (depending on your settings)
- Great for **chapter writing, editing, outlining, dialogue, and research simulation**

Ideal for: Serious writers, course creators, content developers, or anyone writing a full book

Why the Paid Version Is Worth It (Especially for Authors)

If you're using ChatGPT as a co-writing partner, GPT-4 will:

- **Save you hours** of time refining prompts or rewriting weak content
- **Hold structure and tone** over longer interactions
- **Understand your instructions faster** with fewer corrections
- Provide **cleaner, more usable drafts** right out of the gate

"If you're writing a full book with ChatGPT, the $20/month is like hiring an assistant that never gets tired — and always listens."

How to Upgrade (If You Choose To)

1. Log into chat.openai.com
2. Click your name or the ☰ menu
3. Select "Upgrade to Plus"
4. Follow the payment steps — you can cancel any time

Final Tip: You Don't Need to Pay — But You'll Want To

This book will show you how to get great results with **any version** of ChatGPT. But if you plan to write multiple books, create content for clients, or want the best possible responses with less editing, the Plus version is a worthwhile upgrade.

"Think of it like choosing between a good pen and a great one — both will write the book. But one will glide, flow, and follow your lead with ease."
— Dr. Constance Santego

"Writing with AI doesn't silence the author's voice — it amplifies the vision behind it."

— *Dr. Constance Santego*

Introduction

Why AI is a Game-Changer for Writers

We are living through a quiet revolution — one that isn't replacing storytellers, but redefining how we tell our stories.

Artificial intelligence, once confined to sci-fi novels and distant tech labs, now sits beside us at the desk — not as a competitor, but as a co-creator. For authors, this marks a profound shift in the creative process. Suddenly, a blank page isn't lonely. It's filled with possibility.

So why is AI, and specifically ChatGPT, such a game-changer for writers?

1. It Destroys Writer's Block

One of the greatest enemies of authorship is the overwhelming pressure of starting — the paralyzing moment when the mind goes blank, the cursor blinks, and the doubt creeps in. With ChatGPT, inspiration is never more than a prompt away. Whether you need an opening line, a chapter title, or 10 fresh angles for your next idea, the spark is instant.

2. It Accelerates the Creative Process

AI doesn't replace your creativity — it fuels it. Instead of spending days outlining or researching, you can use ChatGPT to generate structures, themes, timelines, and even dialogue. This frees you to focus on the heart of your work: your voice, your story, your message.

3. It Makes High-Level Brainstorming Effortless

Need 50 nonfiction chapter ideas? Want to explore 3 different endings? Curious about metaphors that suit your theme? With AI, you're no longer brainstorming alone. ChatGPT becomes your round-the-clock writing room, creative sounding board, and idea machine.

4. It Helps All Writers — Not Just Professionals

Whether you're writing your first children's book or your tenth novel, AI levels the playing field. It supports beginners who need guidance and offers experts a shortcut to clarity and refinement. The intimidation of the process fades, and accessibility rises.

5. It Supports Every Stage of the Book Journey

From concept to creation, editing to marketing, AI can help every step of the way. It's not just about writing content — it's about naming your book, crafting your author bio, building your back cover copy, finding keywords for publishing platforms, and even outlining your launch strategy.

6. It Empowers Independence

In an industry that can feel gatekept or out of reach, ChatGPT puts tools in your hands that used to cost thousands in consulting, editing, or coaching. With the right prompts, you gain access to insight, structure, strategy — and even emotional encouragement.

In the chapters ahead, you'll learn exactly how to work with ChatGPT in a way that enhances your creativity, honors your voice, and helps you finish the book you were meant to write.

This is the beginning of a new kind of authorship — intuitive, empowered, and supported by intelligent tools designed to help you bring your story to life.

"AI doesn't take away the soul of writing — it clears the clutter so the soul can shine."

WHAT CHATGPT IS (AND WHAT IT ISN'T)

In recent years, "ChatGPT" has become a buzzword — praised, feared, misunderstood, and, for many authors, completely mystifying. But before we dive into how to use it as your writing partner, let's get clear on **what ChatGPT actually is… and what it isn't.**

What ChatGPT Is

A Language Model

ChatGPT is a type of artificial intelligence called a **language model** — specifically a *Generative Pre-trained Transformer*. It's been trained on billions of words from books, websites, research papers, and conversations to learn how humans communicate. It doesn't "think" like we do — but it knows how to *respond* like we do.

A Tool for Generating Ideas and Text

At its core, ChatGPT can help you **generate content** — ideas, outlines, dialogue, metaphors, structure, marketing copy, research summaries, and more. It mimics patterns in language to give you useful outputs based on your prompts.

An Interactive Brainstorming Partner

It works like a conversation — meaning you can give it instructions, correct it, build on its answers, and refine the output until it fits your vision. It's like having a very fast, very knowledgeable writing assistant who never gets tired.

A Powerful Companion in the Creative Process

From plot development to character arcs, from rewriting awkward sentences to suggesting book titles or back cover blurbs,

ChatGPT helps writers move from stuck to inspired — especially when used strategically.

What ChatGPT Isn't

A Human Being or Creative Genius

ChatGPT doesn't have emotions, personal experience, or intuition. It doesn't "understand" in the way humans do — it recognizes *patterns* in language, not meaning. The real creative genius is still **you**.

A Replacement for Your Voice

If you let it, ChatGPT can take over your writing style — but that's not the goal. Used properly, it *amplifies* your voice, not replaces it. You're still the author. The storyteller. The soul behind the book.

Always Accurate

While it sounds confident, ChatGPT can be **wrong**. It can invent facts, misquote sources, and offer information that sounds good but isn't true. That's why human judgment is essential — especially when writing nonfiction, health advice, or educational material.

A Shortcut to Success

AI can speed up your process, but it can't replace discipline, editing, intuition, or storytelling skill. It's not a "get published quick" machine — it's a co-creative partner that helps you work smarter, not lazier.

Think of ChatGPT as Your Writing Mirror

It reflects what you put into it. If your prompt is vague, the output will be vague. If your input is clear, specific, and aligned with your vision, ChatGPT becomes a powerful amplifier of your message.

"ChatGPT is not here to write for you — it's here to write *with* you."

Ethics, Limitations & Boundaries

Co-Creation with Integrity

The use of AI in writing brings exciting possibilities — but it also brings responsibility.

As authors, we carry the weight of influence. What we write has the power to inform, inspire, and shape how people see the world. So when we choose to integrate artificial intelligence into our creative process, it's important to understand not just *what* we can do — but *how* to do it ethically.

1. AI Is a Tool, Not a Ghostwriter

While ChatGPT can write convincing paragraphs, stories, or entire articles, ethical use means remaining the **primary creator**. When you publish a book with AI-assisted content, it should still reflect your **intentions, values, and unique voice**.

Think of it like hiring an editor or brainstorming with a mentor. AI can assist — but *you* are the author.

2. Disclose When It Matters

There's no rule (yet) requiring authors to disclose AI assistance, especially for idea generation, outlines, or minor edits. But if large portions of your content are directly AI-generated without deep revision, **transparency builds trust.**

- For nonfiction or educational books, consider a short acknowledgment of AI assistance.
- For fiction, it may not be necessary unless readers ask — but be ready to own your process with integrity.

3. Know the Limitations

Despite its power, ChatGPT:

- **Can hallucinate facts** (make things up)
- **Does not cite real-time or scholarly sources**
- **Lacks personal experience, emotion, or context**
- **Should never be used to impersonate others** or pass off false information

Always double-check facts, refine voice, and apply your judgment.

4. Don't Use AI to Replicate or Imitate Other Authors

While ChatGPT can mimic style, it's unethical to ask it to "write like [famous author]" and pass that work off as original.
Respecting **intellectual property and creative identity** is part of honoring the literary community.

5. Protect Sensitive & Personal Information

Avoid inputting confidential or private information about yourself or others. While ChatGPT does not retain individual data between sessions, always **treat it like a public space** — especially when discussing clients, real-life stories, or medical/legal information.

6. Respect Cultural & Spiritual Integrity

If you're using ChatGPT to help write about traditional knowledge, spiritual practices, or cultural stories, proceed with **cultural sensitivity**. Always ask:

- *Is this mine to tell?*
- *Am I representing this truthfully and respectfully?*

AI doesn't have discernment — but *you* do.

7. Establish Personal Boundaries With AI Use

Every author must decide:

- How much is too much?
- Where does inspiration end and outsourcing begin?
- Am I still learning, growing, and connecting with my writing — or just generating content?

If using AI begins to dull your joy or disconnect you from your craft, it may be time to pause and reassess.

"Ethical writing isn't about perfection — it's about presence. About knowing why you're creating, and staying aligned with that truth."

Legalities: Copyright, Plagiarism & Disclosure

What Every Author Needs to Know

AI-generated content lives in a legal gray zone — not because it's unethical by nature, but because the laws are still catching up.

As an author using ChatGPT, it's important to understand where **you stand** when it comes to copyright, originality, and ownership.

1. Who Owns AI-Generated Content?

Currently, content created by ChatGPT **cannot hold copyright on its own** — because AI is not a person.
That means:
→ If **you** craft the prompts, refine the responses, and integrate the content into your own work, **you own the copyright**.
→ If you copy-paste and publish large blocks of AI content with no meaningful human input, the originality — and therefore legal protection — may be questioned.

Best Practice: Use ChatGPT as a collaborator, not a replacement. Your intention, editing, and voice matter.

2. Is Using AI Considered Plagiarism?

Not inherently. ChatGPT doesn't pull text directly from other authors or websites. It **generates original responses** based on patterns in its training data.

However:

- If you ask it to write "in the style of" a specific person and then publish that without acknowledgment, that could cross ethical or legal lines.

- If AI unintentionally mimics copyrighted phrasing (rare but possible), and you don't revise or check it, you could end up with unintended duplication.

Best Practice: Treat AI content like you would a draft from a student or ghostwriter — review, revise, and **make it your own** before publishing.

3. Do I Have to Disclose That I Used ChatGPT?

There's no law (at the time of writing) that says you must disclose AI use in your book.
But consider:

- If your readers value transparency, a short note in the acknowledgments can build trust.
- If your content is educational, medical, spiritual, or instructive, readers may appreciate knowing how it was created.

Best Practice: Disclosure isn't always necessary — but *alignment* is. If you're proud of your process and confident in your authorship, you'll know when (and how) to share.

4. What About Publisher Guidelines?

Some traditional publishers, contest rules, or educational platforms now ask about AI involvement. Be honest when submitting — **policies vary widely**, but being upfront protects your integrity and avoids complications down the line.

Best Practice: If in doubt, ask before submitting.

Final Thought: AI + Human = Authorship

You are not violating the creative process by using AI.
You are adapting it.
So long as you:

- Stay involved,
- Refine the work,
- And ensure what you publish reflects your *intent and originality…*

You remain the rightful author.

"AI doesn't remove your authorship — it challenges you to become more conscious of it."

Myths About AI in Creative Writing

What It's Not... and What It Really Can Be

When writers first hear about using AI in the creative process, reactions often fall into one of two extremes: curiosity or concern. And behind those reactions? A wave of assumptions that simply aren't true.

Let's clear the air and bust the biggest myths — so you can step into co-creation with clarity, confidence, and integrity.

MYTH #1: "AI will replace writers."

TRUTH: Writers who use AI as a tool will replace writers who fear it.
AI can assist with brainstorming, structure, and speed — but it can't replicate lived experience, intuition, or human soul. *Books still need a human heart.* Always will.

Think of AI as a brush. The story still needs a painter.

MYTH #2: "If I use AI, it's cheating."

TRUTH: Is using a spellchecker cheating? What about a thesaurus?
Tools don't invalidate creativity — they **support** it. As long as you're guiding the process, making decisions, and shaping the message, you are still 100% the author.

MYTH #3: "AI content is generic and soulless."

TRUTH: It *can* be — if your prompts are.
ChatGPT reflects the clarity and depth of your input. When you bring personal insight, emotion, and purpose to the conversation, the results can be beautifully tailored. It's not about whether AI can write — it's about *how* you use it.

MYTH #4: "Using AI means I'm not a real writer."

TRUTH: Being a "real writer" isn't about suffering through every word.
It's about sharing a message that matters. If AI helps you get that message out of your head and into the world — faster, clearer, and with greater impact — then you're not less of a writer. You're an *empowered one.*

MYTH #5: "AI can write an entire book without me."

TRUTH: It can generate words — but not wisdom.
Without your voice, values, and vision, the output is hollow. AI can help you write a book. But only *you* can write **your** book.

MYTH #6: "AI will make everything sound the same."

TRUTH: Repetition happens when authors don't revise or personalize.
ChatGPT can suggest content quickly, but *your edits, direction, and voice* are what make the final product shine. Treat it like a starting point — not a finished product.

"The only thing artificial about AI is the fear that it can replace the human soul."

How to Prompt Like a Pro

The Art of Asking ChatGPT the Right Way
Basics + Advanced Techniques for Authors

At the heart of every successful interaction with ChatGPT is a well-crafted prompt.
Not magic. Not luck. Just **clarity** + **intention**.

The quality of the answer you receive is only as good as the quality of the question you ask. In other words: *prompting is an art.* And once you learn it, you unlock an entirely new level of creative power.

THE BASICS: FOUNDATIONS OF GOOD PROMPTING

Think of ChatGPT as a writing assistant who is brilliant but needs direction. If you say, "Write me something," it might give you something — but probably not what you want.

A strong prompt includes the following elements:

1. Context — What are you working on?

"I'm writing a nonfiction book for holistic practitioners…"

2. Intent — What do you want ChatGPT to do?

"Can you outline ten chapter topics?"

3. Tone or Style (Optional but Powerful)

"In a warm, encouraging tone, suitable for new practitioners."

4. Format — What should the answer look like?

"List form, with a short description for each."

Basic Prompt Formula:

"I'm working on [PROJECT]. Can you help me [TASK], in a [TONE/STYLE], and give the answer in [FORMAT]?"

Prompting Tips for Beginners

- Be specific: "Give me 5 titles for a cozy mystery set in a bakery" yields better results than "Give me book titles."
- Add context: Tell it who you are, who your readers are, or what your goal is.
- Give examples: "Make this sound like the writing style of Brené Brown (but do not copy her)."
- Stack your requests: You can keep refining results in a back-and-forth flow. Think *conversation*, not command.

Advanced Prompting Techniques (For Masterful Results)

Once you're confident with basic prompting, you can begin to **chain instructions** or set up entire writing sessions like a pro.

1. Role Assignment

"Act as my developmental editor. I'll paste a draft, and I'd like feedback on structure, clarity, and pacing."

This tells ChatGPT *how* to behave and *what lens* to use.

2. Layered Prompting (Prompt Stacking)

Break complex tasks into parts and build on the output.

Example:

1. "Give me 10 chapter titles for a book about self-healing with Reiki."
2. "Now outline Chapter 3 in detail."
3. "Now write the opening paragraph in a poetic tone."

This gives you *cohesive, focused results* — one layer at a time.

3. Input Templates

Use structured input to control tone, length, and detail.

Example Prompt Template:

"You are a spiritual book coach helping me develop a chapter called 'Energy and Intuition.' Write 3 possible introductions (around 150 words each), each in a different tone: poetic, conversational, and scientific."

4. Persona Embedding

Set the stage by feeding it your brand, audience, or writing voice.

Example:

"I am Dr. Constance Santego, a Doctor of Natural Medicine and Reiki Master. My readers are healers, seekers, and teachers. My writing style is direct, encouraging, and rooted in sacred wisdom. Please help me write a book introduction for this audience."

Now everything that follows is **aligned** with your message and market.

Best Practices for Prompting

- Don't be afraid to *correct* it. Say: "Make it warmer," or "Too vague — can you go deeper?"
- Save your best prompts in a document or app. Reuse and refine them.
- Keep a "voice style" paragraph about yourself handy to feed into future prompts.

"The secret to working with ChatGPT isn't having the perfect words — it's knowing how to ask better questions."

CHAPTER 1: Getting Started with Your Book Idea

Brainstorming Book Topics with ChatGPT

From Blank Page to Inspired Direction

Every book begins with a spark — a single question, insight, or moment of curiosity. But when the spark is buried under doubt or too many options, it helps to have a brainstorming partner who never runs out of ideas.

That's where ChatGPT comes in.

Using the right prompts, you can explore **dozens of book ideas in minutes**, tailored to your interests, expertise, and goals. Whether you're starting from nothing or refining a vague concept, ChatGPT can help you quickly find the direction that feels aligned, purposeful, and marketable.

Start With Who You Are

Before you ask ChatGPT for ideas, tell it a little about yourself. The more context you give, the more accurate and inspiring the results.

Try This Prompt:

"I'm a holistic health practitioner with 20+ years of experience in Reiki, natural medicine, and teaching. I'd like to write a book that reflects my expertise. Can you suggest 10 nonfiction book ideas that would interest both practitioners and beginners?"

Or for fiction:

"I'm fascinated by energy healing, spiritual gifts, and reincarnation. Can you brainstorm 10 fiction book ideas that weave these themes into a contemporary setting?"

Refine by Genre or Audience

Don't just say "book idea." Tell ChatGPT:

- The **genre** you're thinking about (self-help, memoir, mystery, fantasy, children's)
- The **audience** you want to serve (women 40+, empaths, entrepreneurs, kids 6–8)
- Your **desired outcome** (inspire, teach, entertain, heal)

Example Prompt:

"I want to write a self-help book for women in midlife who are rediscovering their purpose. Suggest 5 original book titles with themes of spirituality and empowerment."

Fiction Variation:

"I want to write a children's book (ages 4–6) that introduces the idea of emotions and energy in a magical, gentle way. Can you generate 5 unique story concepts?"

Brainstorming Styles: Choose Your Flow

List Format:

"Give me a list of 25 possible book topics for someone with experience in…"
Best for: Quick inspiration or large variety.

Expanded Ideas with Descriptions:

"Can you list 5 book ideas and describe the theme, audience, and unique angle of each?"
Best for: Evaluating viability.

Compare and Choose:

"Here are 3 ideas I'm considering. Help me compare them in terms of originality, audience demand, and ease of writing."

Make It Personal — Then Practical

Once you have a few ideas you like, ask follow-up questions like:

- "Which of these ideas has the most potential for impact?"
- "Can you suggest a subtitle that would appeal to readers in this niche?"
- "What problems does this book solve for the reader?"

Prompt Templates to Try

For Nonfiction:

"I help [group] with [what] so they can [result]. Can you suggest book ideas that align with this?"
"List 10 book topics for someone with expertise in [your field], written in a warm, practical tone."

For Fiction:

"Create 10 story ideas that combine [genre] with [theme], with a female lead character."
"Brainstorm magical realism plot ideas involving past lives, spiritual gifts, or hidden truths."

For Memoir or Mixed:

"I've lived through [your story in one sentence]. What kind of memoir or teaching memoir could I write from this?"
"Suggest hybrid book structures that mix personal story with teaching points."

"When you're not sure what to write, don't ask what's trending — ask what's *true* to you. Then let ChatGPT help shape it into something the world needs."

Genre-Specific Idea Generation

Fiction, Nonfiction, Children's, Memoir, and Beyond

Once you know you want to write a book, the next big question is: *What kind of book should it be?* Your genre shapes everything — from structure and tone to audience expectations and marketing potential.

Using ChatGPT, you can generate tailored book ideas in *any* genre — and even blend genres to discover unique concepts that reflect your voice and vision.

FICTION

From fantasy epics to cozy mysteries, fiction is where imagination leads. ChatGPT is especially helpful in generating:

- Plot archetypes (hero's journey, forbidden love, mystery unravels, etc.)
- Genre-specific tropes (e.g., "grumpy meets sunshine" for romance)
- High-stakes conflicts and character arcs
- Unique settings and magical systems

Try These Prompts:

"Create 5 plot ideas for a metaphysical romance set in modern-day Italy."
"Give me 3 character-driven story ideas that combine healing energy and reincarnation."
"I want to write a magical realism novel. Generate titles and themes rooted in spiritual awakening."

NONFICTION

Nonfiction ideas are often born from *experience, expertise,* or a desire to *teach, inspire, or guide* others.

ChatGPT can help you:

- Identify what you're qualified to write
- Turn your method, story, or teaching into a framework
- Brainstorm solutions-focused titles and themes
- Align your idea with your reader's needs

Try These Prompts:

"I help people [do what]. Suggest 10 nonfiction book ideas I could write."
"What problems do new Reiki practitioners face, and how could I write a book to solve one of them?"
"Suggest book titles for a spiritual guidebook about transforming pain into purpose."

CHILDREN'S BOOKS

Children's books require simplicity, heart, and often a touch of wonder. ChatGPT can help generate:

- Stories appropriate to age level
- Rhyming concepts or moral lessons
- Magical but gentle narratives
- Educational angles for parents and teachers

Try These Prompts:

"Generate 3 story ideas for a picture book (ages 3–6) about emotions and energy healing."
"List titles for a children's book series teaching mindfulness and nature connection."

"Write a brief story concept about a dragon who teaches kids how to feel safe with big feelings."

MEMOIR & HYBRID

Memoirs walk the line between personal and universal. You can also blend memoir with teaching (common in the healing, business, or spiritual space).

ChatGPT can help you:

- Identify the central theme of your story
- Structure personal experiences into teachable moments
- Explore hybrid options (story + workbook, memoir + lessons)

Try These Prompts:

"I've lived through [brief story]. Suggest memoir or teaching memoir structures I could use."
"What themes could be drawn from surviving [life event] that would help others heal?"
"Generate a working title and subtitle for a transformational memoir about awakening psychic gifts after grief."

CROSS-GENRE & SPIRITUAL WRITING

Your work may blend nonfiction wisdom with storytelling, or children's messages with energy medicine. That's where ChatGPT shines — helping you explore *cross-genre innovation.*

Try This Prompt:

"Give me 5 cross-genre book ideas that combine spiritual growth, creative writing, and practical self-help."

BONUS TIP: Use ChatGPT to Identify Your Genre

If you're unsure what genre your idea fits in, ask:

"Here's my book idea: [insert concept]. What genre(s) would this fall under, and how might I best structure it?"

"Genre isn't a box. It's a doorway. Once you name it, you can play with it, expand it, or break the rules — but first, you have to know what room you're in."

Evaluating Market Demand

Writing What You Love — That Others Want to Read

Choosing a topic you're passionate about is essential — but if you want your book to *sell*, it also needs to resonate with readers. That's where market demand comes in.

Using ChatGPT, you can quickly assess whether your book idea aligns with what people are *searching for, struggling with,* or *excited to buy.*

This isn't about chasing trends.
It's about aligning your message with a real audience need.

WHY MARKET DEMAND MATTERS

Writing a book takes time and energy — and publishing it means stepping into a marketplace. If you're hoping to grow your brand, income, or impact, then knowing what readers *want* (and where your book fits in) is empowering, not limiting.

Market demand helps you:

- Validate your book concept
- Shape your title and subtitle
- Tailor your chapters to solve reader problems
- Improve visibility on Amazon and online bookstores

HOW CHATGPT CAN HELP

While ChatGPT doesn't access live Amazon or Google keyword data, it can *simulate trends and reader behavior* based on patterns. Use it to:

1. Identify Pain Points and Reader Desires

Prompt Example:

"What are the top 10 problems people face when trying to start a spiritual healing business?"
"What questions do first-time authors ask before writing a book?"

This gives you insight into what your audience *cares about* — and how your book can help.

2. Analyze Comparable Titles

Prompt Example:

"List 5 bestselling books similar to [your idea]. What topics do they cover? What's their tone?"
"What themes are trending in women's self-help books today?"

Ask ChatGPT to help you study what's working in your niche — so you can carve out your unique space.

3. Generate Keyword Ideas

Prompt Example:

"Suggest 15 keywords and phrases people might search for related to [your book topic]."

These keywords help later when you:

- Create your subtitle
- Write your back cover
- Upload to Amazon or IngramSpark

4. Refine Your Book Idea Based on Demand

Prompt Example:

"Here's my idea: [Insert your concept]. How could I refine or position this to better match current reader interest?"

ChatGPT might suggest shifting your audience slightly, adding a trending theme, or narrowing the focus — all while keeping your core message intact.

Best Practices for Evaluating Demand

- Ask ChatGPT for simulated market insight — then verify using real tools like Publisher Rocket, Google Trends, or Amazon searches.
- Don't lose your voice to trends. Instead, *frame your truth* in a way that helps solve real problems.
- Revisit your audience description often — if you wouldn't read the book you're writing, chances are others won't either.

Is My Book Market-Ready?

A Quick-Check Before You Start Writing

Use this checklist to clarify if your book idea is aligned with your goals *and* with the needs of your ideal reader.

IDEA CLARITY

- I know what my book is about — in one or two clear sentences.
- I've chosen a genre or cross-genre that fits my message and audience.

- I can describe what makes this book *different* or *special* from others in the same space.

AUDIENCE ALIGNMENT

- I know who I'm writing for (demographics, mindset, challenges, desires).
- I've identified a specific problem, question, or experience my reader is seeking help or resonance with.
- I can name 1–3 books my ideal reader may have already read — and what mine adds.

MARKET INSIGHT

- I've asked ChatGPT to help identify keywords, themes, and related titles.
- I've considered how my book can be positioned for impact or discoverability.
- I know whether I'm writing this to teach, inspire, entertain, build my brand, or all of the above.

MESSAGING + HOOK

- I've written (or started crafting) a short elevator pitch.
- I've experimented with book hooks or subtitles using ChatGPT prompts.
- I feel confident this book has *both* personal meaning and reader relevance.

If you've checked most of these boxes — congratulations! You're ready to move from **idea to outline** in the next chapter.

"Write from your soul — but aim with strategy. Your message deserves to be heard by the people who need it most."

Creating an Elevator Pitch or Book Hook

Capture Attention. Share the Heart. Spark Curiosity.

Before you write your first chapter — and long before you hit "publish" — you need to be able to answer one simple question:

"What's your book about?"

This is where your **elevator pitch** or **book hook** comes in. Whether you're pitching to a publisher, speaking to your audience, or promoting your book online, a clear, powerful hook can make the difference between someone scrolling past — or leaning in.

And with ChatGPT, crafting one becomes easy, collaborative, and surprisingly creative.

WHAT'S AN ELEVATOR PITCH?

Your **elevator pitch** is a short, compelling summary of your book that tells:

- **What it's about**
- **Who it's for**
- **What transformation or experience it offers**

It should be **1–3 sentences max** and sound natural when spoken.

"It's a practical guide for intuitive entrepreneurs who want to scale their healing business using energy alignment and grounded strategy."

"It's a novel about a woman who inherits her grandmother's apothecary and unlocks an ancestral gift that forces her to choose between the past and her purpose."

WHAT'S A BOOK HOOK?

Your **book hook** is more emotional. It's the *"why should I care?"* It evokes curiosity, desire, or emotional connection.

"What if the AI helping you write your book was also helping you heal your story?"

"She thought she came to the vineyard to write about wine. She didn't expect to rewrite her life."

A great hook can also double as your **social media caption, back cover opener**, or even a **subtitle.**

Using ChatGPT to Write a Hook or Pitch

Start with This Prompt:

"I'm writing a [genre] book for [audience]. The main idea is [core theme or transformation]. Can you write 3 short elevator pitches and 3 hooks that I can use in my marketing?"

Example Input:

"I'm writing a nonfiction book for aspiring authors who want to use ChatGPT to write, edit, and publish their books faster and with more confidence."

Output Might Be:
Elevator Pitch:

1. "A practical guide to using AI as your writing partner, from blank page to published book."
2. "This book teaches authors how to co-create with ChatGPT without losing their voice."
3. "Everything you need to brainstorm, structure, write, and sell your book — with the help of AI."

Hooks:

1. "You're not behind — you're just one prompt away from momentum."
2. "Write faster. Write better. Write with AI by your side."
3. "The future of authorship isn't artificial — it's *amplified*."

Prompt Variations for Better Results

- "Rewrite this pitch to make it more emotional/intriguing/conversational."
- "Make this hook more spiritual/inspiring/playful."
- "Add a transformation outcome to this sentence."
- "Turn this idea into a back cover teaser."

Final Tip: Make It Yours

Even if ChatGPT gives you something great, always tweak it until it feels like *your* voice. Your hook is not just a marketing tool — it's the soul of your book in miniature.

"A good hook captures attention. A great one captures the truth."

Prompt Examples:

"Help me brainstorm…" / "Generate 10 book ideas…"

Real Prompts to Spark Real Books

Now that you understand how to craft a strong book idea — and how to assess its audience and market potential — it's time to practice the skill that will carry you through your entire writing journey: **prompting.**

Below are ready-to-use prompt examples you can customize based on your genre, message, and goals. You'll find variations for nonfiction, fiction, children's books, memoir, and cross-genre works.

NONFICTION BOOK IDEA PROMPTS

"Help me brainstorm 10 nonfiction book ideas for women over 40 seeking spiritual renewal."

"Generate 10 practical book titles for a natural medicine practitioner who teaches energy healing."

"List 5 book ideas that combine business strategy with intuitive development for heart-centered entrepreneurs."

"What are some creative angles I could use to write a beginner's guide to Reiki that hasn't been done before?"

FICTION BOOK IDEA PROMPTS

"Give me 10 story ideas that blend reincarnation, healing, and past-life romance."

"Help me brainstorm a fantasy novel with a female lead who discovers her psychic abilities in a modern world."

"Generate 3 magical realism story ideas that explore grief and transformation through ancestral memories."

"I want to write a cozy mystery with metaphysical themes. Can you suggest settings, plot ideas, and quirky characters?"

CHILDREN'S BOOK IDEA PROMPTS

"Give me 5 story ideas for a picture book (ages 4–7) that teaches children how to identify and release emotions."

"Generate 10 titles for a children's book series about animals who represent the 5 elements (wood, fire, earth, metal, water)."

"Help me create a simple story concept that introduces mindfulness and breathwork to kids in a fun, magical way."

MEMOIR & TEACHING MEMOIR PROMPTS

"I overcame [brief life challenge]. What kind of memoir or transformation-based book could I write to inspire others?"

"Help me brainstorm 3 structures for combining my personal healing journey with lessons I now teach as a practitioner."

"Suggest titles and chapter ideas for a memoir about finding faith through grief, using intuitive gifts."

CROSS-GENRE & HYBRID PROMPTS

"I want to write a part-workbook, part-teaching book, part-story. Can you help me structure it and suggest a unique angle?"

"Combine my interests in holistic health, ancient wisdom, and emotional healing into a compelling nonfiction book idea."

"Suggest 5 unique formats for a book that's part oracle, part journal, and part spiritual guide."

Final Prompt Template

Here's a universal plug-and-play template:

"I am a [your role/expertise], and I want to write a [type of book] for [your audience]. The theme is [key idea]. Can you generate 10 book ideas or titles that blend my experience with what my readers are looking for?"

"Don't wait for the perfect idea to land in your lap. Ask for it. Shape it. Prompt it into existence."

CHAPTER 2: Planning Your Book

Structuring Your Book by Genre

Turning Your Idea Into a Clear, Compelling Framework

Once you have your idea, the next step is to **build the structure** — the bones that will hold your book together. The right structure not only gives your writing direction, but also ensures your message lands clearly with your readers.

Different genres have different expectations. A memoir is not structured like a how-to guide. A children's book flows differently than a novel. The more you understand genre-specific frameworks, the more you can use ChatGPT to help you outline and organize your book effectively.

NONFICTION STRUCTURE (Teaching, Self-Help, How-To)

These books are designed to inform, inspire, or transform. The structure is usually *problem-solution* focused.

Common Frameworks:

- **Linear Teaching Model:** Start from beginner to advanced (step-by-step guide)
- **Problem → Insight → Solution:** Each chapter tackles a specific challenge

- **Framework-Based:** Introduce a concept (e.g., 5 steps, 7 pillars), then devote a chapter to each

Use ChatGPT to Prompt:

"Outline a nonfiction book that teaches [topic] to [audience], structured around 7 key principles."

"Create a 10-chapter structure that walks readers through a personal transformation related to [theme]."

FICTION STRUCTURE (Novels, Short Stories)

Fiction relies on **narrative arc**, character development, and emotional pacing.

Most Common Fiction Structures:

- **Three-Act Structure:** Setup → Confrontation → Resolution
- **Hero's Journey:** Call to adventure → Ordeal → Transformation → Return
- **Save the Cat Beat Sheet:** 15 plot points used by screenwriters and novelists

Use ChatGPT to Prompt:

"Structure a fantasy novel using the Hero's Journey with a female protagonist discovering her healing gift."

"Create a 3-act outline for a romance where the two leads are spiritual opposites."

CHILDREN'S BOOK STRUCTURE

(Ages 3–8 picture books or early readers)

Children's books require simplicity, rhythm, repetition, and clarity of message.

Typical Format:

- **Beginning:** Introduce character + problem
- **Middle:** Escalating emotional or situational tension
- **End:** Resolution with a gentle lesson or insight

For rhythmic or rhyming books: 28–32 pages, often 12–16 spreads.

Use ChatGPT to Prompt:

"Structure a picture book (ages 4–6) that teaches kids how to recognize emotions using a forest animal character."

"Give me a page-by-page outline for a 32-page story about a magical garden that teaches breathwork."

MEMOIR STRUCTURE

(Traditional or Teaching Memoir)

Memoir isn't just "what happened" — it's about the **emotional truth** beneath the events. The best memoirs have narrative flow *and* thematic focus.

Common Approaches:

- **Chronological:** Follows your life or event from beginning to end
- **Fragmented or Thematic:** Stories grouped around a topic (grief, healing, freedom)
- **Hybrid Memoir + Teaching:** One story, then one takeaway (often used in spiritual or coaching-based books)

Use ChatGPT to Prompt:

"Structure a memoir that blends personal awakening with teachings on intuitive development."

"Help me outline a hybrid memoir about overcoming trauma through Reiki."

HYBRID OR CROSS-GENRE STRUCTURE

More and more authors are blending genres. Your book might be:

- Half teaching, half story
- A journal and guidebook
- A workbook and spiritual manual
- Fiction with real-world wisdom woven in

Use ChatGPT to Prompt:

"Help me structure a hybrid book that includes personal stories, exercises, and oracle-style reflections."

"Can you combine fiction and nonfiction in a structure that teaches energy medicine while telling a story?"

Final Tip: Always Start With the Reader's Journey

Ask yourself:

- What does the reader *start with* (a question, pain point, desire)?
- What do you want them to *feel, learn, or realize* by the end?
- Then, ask ChatGPT:

"What is the best structure to take the reader from [starting point] to [desired transformation]?"

"Structure doesn't restrict creativity — it gives it direction. Once you build the container, your message can truly flow."

Fiction: Plot Archetypes, Characters, Conflict, Themes

Building a Story That Moves, Matters, and Lasts

Fiction is alchemy — the blend of imagination, emotion, and structure. But even the most intuitive writers benefit from frameworks that guide the storytelling process. With ChatGPT as your partner, you can create compelling fiction that follows classic storytelling arcs while remaining uniquely your own.

Let's explore the key ingredients of great fiction and how to generate each one with AI.

1. Plot Archetypes: Universal Story Foundations

Plot archetypes are timeless storytelling patterns that resonate across cultures and genres. They serve as the skeleton your narrative can grow around.

Common Fiction Archetypes:

- **The Quest** – A hero journeys to achieve a goal or retrieve something of value (*The Lord of the Rings*)
- **Overcoming the Monster** – Facing internal or external threats (*Beowulf, Dracula*)
- **Rags to Riches** – A transformation from humble beginnings to greatness (*Cinderella*)
- **The Journey Inward** – A spiritual or emotional evolution (*Eat, Pray, Love*)
- **The Forbidden Love** – Love that must survive outside pressures (*Romeo and Juliet*)

ChatGPT Prompt Example:

"List 7 possible storylines based on the 'Overcoming the Monster' archetype, but make the 'monster' symbolic — like fear, grief, or unworthiness."

"Help me choose the best plot archetype for a novel about a healer unlocking her ancestral gifts."

2. Character Development: Deep, Relatable, Real

Memorable fiction lives through its characters. Readers don't follow plots — they follow people. You can use ChatGPT to generate character profiles, motivations, flaws, and arcs.

Key Character Questions:

- What do they want — and what do they *need*?
- What wound are they carrying?
- How will they change by the end?

Prompt Examples:

"Create a character profile for a reluctant psychic in her 40s who's hiding her gifts after a traumatic childhood."

"What are 5 possible character arcs for a spiritual detective solving crimes with intuitive abilities?"

You can also ask:

"What does this character fear most?"
"Who or what challenges their worldview?"
"How could their backstory shape their current flaw?"

3. Conflict: The Engine of the Story

Conflict creates tension. Without it, the story stalls. It doesn't have to be dramatic — but it does have to matter.

Types of Conflict:

- **Internal:** Shame, fear, guilt, doubt
- **Interpersonal:** Arguments, betrayal, misunderstanding
- **External:** Threats, survival, societal constraints
- **Philosophical:** Belief systems, moral dilemmas, spiritual dissonance

Prompt Examples:

"What's a believable conflict for a healer in a small town who is secretly working with energy medicine while hiding from her past?"

"Suggest 5 plot complications that could arise in a story about a young empath learning to control her gift."

4. Themes: The Soul of the Story

Themes are what your story *means*. They're the emotional current running beneath the action. With ChatGPT, you can name, shape, and reinforce your themes from the beginning.

Common Fiction Themes:

- Identity
- Healing
- Redemption
- Freedom
- Love vs. Fear
- Trust, Faith, Belonging

Prompt Examples:

"I want to explore the theme of 'self-trust' in a fantasy setting. Suggest character arcs and plot beats that support this."

"What are 3 layered themes I can weave into a novel about a woman discovering her family's hidden lineage of healers?"

Putting It All Together: Integrated Prompts

Once you have a general idea of the story, you can build layered prompts like:

"I want to write a spiritual fiction novel using the 'quest' archetype. The main character is a burned-out therapist who rediscovers her psychic gift after a mysterious client arrives. Can you suggest a 3-act structure, main character arc, conflict, and 2 secondary characters who challenge her beliefs?"

You'll be amazed at how cohesive and complete the results can be — giving you a detailed story seed that can grow into a full manuscript.

"Structure shapes the story. But soul gives it meaning. When you blend both, fiction becomes transformation."

Nonfiction: Outlines, Core Message, Audience Needs

Teach, Inspire, and Transform With Clarity

Nonfiction writing is a sacred exchange: you give your readers knowledge, wisdom, or perspective, and in return, they give you their trust and time.

Whether you're writing a how-to guide, a spiritual teaching manual, a business book, or a wellness memoir, success depends on three things: **clarity of message, alignment with your audience, and a strong structural outline.**

ChatGPT can help you achieve all three.

Your Core Message: What Are You Really Saying?

Every nonfiction book has a **central promise** — the takeaway that your reader walks away with.

Ask yourself (or prompt ChatGPT):

"What is the transformation this book offers my reader?"
"If my book had one sentence of truth, what would it be?"
"How does my personal story or expertise support this message?"

Once your message is clear, every chapter should point back to it — directly or thematically.

Prompt Example:

"I'm writing a book about burnout recovery for energy healers. Help me refine my core message into one strong sentence, and list 3 possible subtitles."

Understanding Your Audience: Speak Directly to Their Needs

Knowing who you're writing for makes the difference between a forgettable book and a life-changing one.

Your audience has:

- **Questions they're asking**
- **Pain points they're trying to solve**
- **Hopes and outcomes they want to experience**

Use ChatGPT to clarify:

"Who would most benefit from a book about [topic]?"
"What emotional tone and language would resonate with [specific audience]?"
"List common misconceptions or struggles this audience faces."

Example:

"My readers are spiritual entrepreneurs who feel overwhelmed by business systems. Suggest chapter topics that address both mindset and practical tools."

Outlining Your Nonfiction Book: 3 Common Structures

1. Step-by-Step (Linear Teaching Model)

Best for how-to, coaching, or instructional books.

- Start with foundational concepts
- Build up to advanced techniques
- End with application or integration

Prompt Example:

"Create a 10-chapter outline for a Reiki training book, from beginner to advanced levels."

2. Problem → Insight → Solution (Transformational)

Best for self-help or spiritual growth.

- Chapter 1–3: Identify pain points
- Chapter 4–6: Offer new frameworks
- Chapter 7–10: Teach implementation or embodiment

Prompt Example:

"Outline a nonfiction book that helps people overcome fear-based thinking through energy awareness and mindset shifts."

3. Framework-Based (Branded Method or Signature System)

Best for thought leaders or teachers with a proprietary model.

- Introduce your system early
- Dedicate a chapter to each pillar
- Conclude with case studies or advanced strategies

Prompt Example:

"I teach a 5-part framework for intuitive development. Help me structure a book that explains each pillar with stories and exercises."

CHAPTER DEVELOPMENT PROMPTS

Once you've chosen your structure, use ChatGPT to build out each chapter.

"Based on the outline we created, give me a breakdown of Chapter 2 including 3 main teaching points, 1 story example, and 1 reflection exercise."

"Write a draft chapter intro in a warm, encouraging tone for beginners."

"Suggest journal prompts that support this chapter's lesson."

Linking Message + Audience + Structure

Master Prompt Example:

"I'm writing a spiritual business book for holistic entrepreneurs who want to scale their income without burning out. The core message is that energy alignment must come before strategy. Help me outline the book, define the audience, and clarify the emotional journey they'll take through each chapter."

"A great nonfiction book doesn't just teach. It understands. It walks with the reader through the unknown — and hands them a map back to themselves."

Children's Books: Age-Appropriate Themes, Language, Illustrations

Creating Magical, Meaningful Stories for Young Readers

Writing a children's book is deceptively simple — short sentences, fewer words, and lots of pictures. But behind that simplicity lies one of the most challenging tasks of all: **speaking to the heart of a child** in a way that is clear, engaging, and emotionally true.

ChatGPT can be an incredible partner in this process — helping you brainstorm concepts, simplify language, and even plan page-by-page structure. But to use it well, you must guide it with age-appropriate expectations.

START WITH THE READER'S AGE GROUP

Children's books vary drastically by age. Each developmental stage requires different:

- Vocabulary levels
- Story lengths
- Attention spans
- Moral and emotional depth
- Illustration needs

Here's a quick breakdown:

Age Group	Book Type	Word Count	Key Features
0–3	Board Books	0–300 words	Rhyming, repetition, basic concepts

Age Group	Book Type	Word Count	Key Features
3–6	Picture Books	300–700 words	Simple plots, big emotions, visual-driven
6–8	Early Readers	800–1500 words	Dialogue, short chapters, mild conflict
8–12	Chapter Books/Middle Grade	5,000–30,000 words	Deeper themes, more complex characters

Common Themes by Age Group

Ages 0–3 (Board Books)

- First words, animals, sounds, shapes
- Bonding, bedtime, feelings
- Simple cause-and-effect

Prompt Example:

"Generate 5 board book ideas for babies that introduce calming bedtime routines through animal characters."

Ages 3–6 (Picture Books)

- Friendship, emotions, sharing, kindness
- Overcoming fear, imagination, nature
- Gentle repetition, conflict resolved quickly

Prompt Example:

"Create a picture book story outline about a shy bunny who learns to express feelings with color magic."

Ages 6–8 (Early Readers)

- Making friends, solving problems, learning from mistakes
- Positive habits, teamwork, honesty
- Beginning to read independently

Prompt Example:

"Outline a short story series for ages 6–8 about a magical school where students learn healing powers from animals."

Ages 8–12 (Middle Grade)

- Identity, belonging, personal growth
- Adventure, mystery, family issues
- Deeper storylines with emotional complexity

Prompt Example:

"Brainstorm 5 middle-grade fiction concepts involving inherited intuition or secret spiritual gifts."

Language: Keep It Clear, Age-Appropriate & Emotionally Resonant

You can use ChatGPT to simplify or adapt your writing for specific reading levels.

Prompt Example:

"Rewrite this paragraph in language suitable for a 5-year-old."

"Can you simplify this story but keep the emotion intact for ages 3–6?"

Also try:

"Turn this story into a rhyming version for toddlers."
"Make this dialogue more playful and natural for young children."

Illustrations: Planning Visuals with AI's Help

Even if you're not the illustrator, ChatGPT can help you map out visuals — especially for picture books.

Prompt Example:

"Create a 12-spread page plan for a picture book, with short descriptions of what should be shown in each illustration."

This is helpful for:

- Creating a book dummy
- Communicating with illustrators
- Planning pacing and visual rhythm

Advanced Prompting Tips for Children's Books

- "Give me a calming bedtime story with natural imagery and a gentle rhythm."
- "Create a character arc for a magical creature who helps kids process big emotions."
- "List animal characters that symbolically represent the 5 elements and their qualities for a children's book series."

Best Practices for Writing Children's Books with ChatGPT

- Always **read aloud** what you've written — children's stories are experienced through sound and rhythm.
- Avoid talking *down* to children — honor their emotional depth while keeping language accessible.
- Use repetition, visual metaphors, and gentle pacing to make your message land.

"Writing for children is not about saying less — it's about saying what matters, simply enough to be remembered forever."

Organizing Research & Reference Prompts

Let ChatGPT Help You Collect, Summarize, and Structure Information Efficiently

Every great book — even fiction — is built on a foundation of **clarity and context**. Whether you're gathering facts, deepening your understanding of a topic, or keeping track of inspirational material, organizing your research is essential.

ChatGPT can't browse the internet (unless you're using a web-enabled version), but it can still help you:

- Generate reference material from known knowledge
- Summarize complex topics
- Organize scattered notes
- Create structured content from raw input

This section will show you how to **use ChatGPT as a research assistant**, helping you make sense of your findings and integrate them into your book with ease.

1. Simulated Research Prompts

Use ChatGPT to simulate known facts, summaries, and historical or conceptual overviews.

Examples:

"Summarize the core principles of Traditional Chinese Medicine in under 300 words for a beginner reader."

"What are the main stages of grief, and how could they be explained in spiritual terms for a healing book?"

"Explain how the subconscious mind stores trauma in simple language, suitable for a self-help book."

This helps you:

- Save time on initial research
- Identify areas where deeper sourcing is needed
- Keep explanations clear and reader-friendly

2. Organizing Raw Notes and Ideas

If you've gathered your own notes, journal entries, or messy content from multiple sources, ChatGPT can help you sort and structure it.

Prompt Examples:

"Here's a list of notes I've collected on chakra balancing. Can you group these into 5–7 themes or chapter topics?"

"Help me organize this list of healing modalities into categories: body-based, energy-based, spiritual, and integrative."

"Turn these bullet points into a cohesive outline for a chapter on emotional detox."

3. Creating Comparison or Summary Tables

For nonfiction, spiritual, or health-based content, you can use ChatGPT to build easy-to-read reference tools.

Prompt Example:

"Create a table comparing Reiki, Reflexology, and Acupuncture — include origin, method, benefits, and spiritual connection."

"Make a chart that compares left-brain vs. right-brain traits and how they relate to creativity and intuition."

These tables can be used directly in your book or as teaching aids in companion courses or workbooks.

4. Citing Sources & Building a Reference List (Caution)

Note: ChatGPT doesn't provide real-time or reliable source citations. It may **invent books, authors, or studies**.

Use prompts like these for organizing citations you already have:

"Here's a list of books I referenced. Organize them into APA format."

"I have citations in messy text. Can you reformat them cleanly for a bibliography?"

You can also ask:

"What type of source should I use to support this claim: 'energy blocks can cause physical illness'?"

5. Supporting Arguments or Insights with AI

Once you've identified a chapter's key points, you can ask ChatGPT to fill in supportive content:

Examples:

"Expand this idea: 'Fear often hides under the surface of anger.' Give me a paragraph with emotional and spiritual depth."

"Write a story or metaphor that explains what it means to be 'energetically misaligned.'"

"Give me 3 simple ways to explain quantum healing for beginners."

Prompting Tips for Research Organization

- Break large topics into parts.
- Ask for bullet points first, then expand.
- Keep a running list of refined prompts that worked well — reuse as needed.
- Use follow-ups like:

    "Add more scientific tone,"
    "Make this more spiritual," or
    "Simplify this for a younger audience."

"Your book doesn't need *everything you know*. It needs *only what serves the reader's journey*. Use AI to find and organize the gold."

Prompt Examples for Creating Book Outlines

Your Blueprint Begins With a Simple Question

Once you've clarified your idea, audience, and genre, the next powerful step is to **outline your book** — and with ChatGPT, you don't have to do it alone. Whether you're writing a how-to guide, a novel, a memoir, or a children's book, your outline becomes your roadmap — helping you stay focused, intentional, and inspired as you write.

Here are **real prompt examples** you can use (or tweak) to generate, revise, and expand your book outline — no matter what kind of book you're creating.

NONFICTION OUTLINE PROMPTS

"I'm writing a book for empaths on how to protect their energy. Can you create a 10-chapter outline that moves from awareness to empowerment?"

"Structure a book using my 5-step healing method. Each chapter should focus on one pillar, with examples and exercises."

"Outline a practical guide for starting a wellness business, including mindset, marketing, legal setup, and client care."

Advanced Add-On:

"Include a suggested introduction and conclusion chapter. Add reflection prompts at the end of each chapter."

FICTION OUTLINE PROMPTS

"Outline a three-act plot for a story about a reiki practitioner who uncovers a hidden spiritual war in her city."

"Using the Hero's Journey, create a 12-step plot structure for a teenage girl who finds a sacred object that awakens her ancestral memory."

"I want to write a cozy mystery with a metaphysical twist. Can you outline 10 chapters with a balance of plot, character development, and spiritual insight?"

Pro Tip:
Ask follow-up questions to expand on chapters:

"Now expand Chapter 3 into 3 scenes."

CHILDREN'S BOOK OUTLINE PROMPTS

"Create a 12-spread outline for a picture book (ages 4–6) about a fox who learns to express sadness using color magic."

"Outline a children's book series for ages 6–8 that teaches emotional regulation through forest animal friends."

"Help me create a page-by-page story plan for a book that introduces kids to the concept of chakras through a garden adventure."

MEMOIR / TEACHING MEMOIR OUTLINE PROMPTS

"I want to write a spiritual memoir about discovering my intuitive gifts after grief. Can you suggest a chapter-by-chapter structure that blends personal story with spiritual lessons?"

"Help me structure a healing memoir that begins with burnout and ends with personal empowerment. Include chapter titles that reflect emotional stages."

"I teach a 7-step process for emotional clearing. Help me outline a hybrid memoir that weaves in my story and teaches this method."

HYBRID & CROSS-GENRE BOOK OUTLINE PROMPTS

"Create a structure for a book that blends storytelling, journal prompts, and energy healing techniques."

"Outline a part oracle, part guidebook that offers spiritual insight, symbolic meaning, and practical action for each chapter."

"I want to write a book that teaches business strategy to holistic practitioners with intuitive prompts and case studies. Help me organize the flow."

Final Prompt Formula
Use this for nearly any genre:

"I am writing a [type of book] for [audience] about [core message or theme]. Can you create a [#]-chapter outline with suggested chapter titles and a short description of what each one will cover?"

"You don't have to start with a blank page. Start with a prompt — and let your outline take shape, one inspired insight at a time."

CHAPTER 3: Writing Chapter by Chapter

Using ChatGPT to Draft a Chapter

From Blank Page to First Draft — One Prompt at a Time

Starting a chapter can feel overwhelming — even with a strong outline. But with ChatGPT as your writing partner, you can move from idea to first draft quickly, creatively, and with much less resistance. The key isn't to let AI take over — it's to let it *jumpstart* your flow.

This section shows you how to use ChatGPT to draft powerful chapter content while keeping your **voice, structure, and purpose** intact.

START WITH STRUCTURE

Before you ask ChatGPT to "write a chapter," give it clear direction.

Include in your prompt:

- Chapter title or theme
- Your intended audience
- Tone or style (warm, professional, poetic, direct, etc.)
- Key points or questions to cover
- Desired length or format (e.g., 800 words, include a story, etc.)

Basic Draft Prompt Example

"Write a first draft for a chapter titled *The Power of Presence'* for a self-help book aimed at spiritual entrepreneurs. The tone should be warm and grounded. Include three key insights about how presence impacts intuition and success, and open with a relatable story or metaphor."

ChatGPT will generate a structured first draft, which you can then:

- Expand
- Reword
- Personalize
- Edit for authenticity and depth

Layered Prompting for a Stronger Draft

Rather than asking for a full chapter at once, break it into pieces.

Step-by-Step Prompt Flow:

1. **"Outline the main points for a chapter on [topic]."**
2. **"Write an opening paragraph that draws the reader in emotionally."**
3. **"Expand on point #1 with a practical example."**
4. **"Summarize the key takeaways from this chapter in an empowering tone."**

This keeps your message clear and lets you shape each section with intention.

Advanced Prompting Techniques

- **Voice Matching:**

"Write this chapter in a style similar to my past writing. Here's a sample paragraph: [insert]. Match tone and flow."

- **Storytelling Enhancement:**

"Add a short, fictional example that illustrates this lesson, suitable for readers who enjoy storytelling."

- **Simplification or Amplification:**

"Rewrite this draft to be more emotionally impactful."
"Make this section more concise and to the point."
"Add spiritual metaphors to deepen the meaning."

Writing WITH ChatGPT, Not Just THROUGH It

Here's the mindset shift:
You are not outsourcing your chapter. You are co-creating it.

Use AI to:

- Break through resistance
- Explore alternate ways of expressing an idea
- Hear your own thoughts reflected back to you with clarity
- Save time on rough drafts, while keeping editing sacred

Your Voice Still Matters Most

No matter how good ChatGPT's draft is, remember:

- Revise to match your lived experience and language
- Insert your truth, your stories, your energy
- Use AI as scaffolding — but *you* are the builder

"The first draft doesn't need to be perfect. It needs to exist. Let ChatGPT help you start — and then shape it into something that's truly yours."

Keeping Voice and Tone Consistent

Maintaining Your Signature Style — Even With AI Support

Your voice is what makes your writing unmistakably yours. It's not just what you say — it's *how* you say it: the rhythm of your sentences, the emotional energy behind your words, and the way your message lands in your reader's heart.

When using ChatGPT to help draft content, it's essential to preserve your **voice and tone**, so the final result still feels authentic, aligned, and resonant. Fortunately, there are simple strategies and prompt techniques that ensure your writing stays *you* — even when co-created with AI.

WHAT IS VOICE VS. TONE?

- **Voice** is your writing personality. It's consistent across everything you create.
- **Tone** is how you speak in a given moment — warm, bold, professional, poetic, etc. It shifts based on your message or mood.

Your goal: Maintain your voice while using tone strategically.

Step 1: Define Your Voice First

Before asking ChatGPT to write anything for you, **tell it who you are**.

Voice Prompt Example:

"I'm Dr. Constance Santego. My writing voice is direct, empowering, spiritual, and grounded in wisdom. I often use metaphors, short impactful lines, and language that blends the sacred with the practical."

You can reuse this as your **"Voice Primer Prompt"** anytime to train ChatGPT on how to respond.

Step 2: Feed It a Sample of Your Writing

ChatGPT can mirror your style with surprising accuracy if you show it what your writing looks like.

Prompt Example:

"Here's a sample paragraph from my previous writing: [paste]. Match this voice and tone in a new paragraph about [topic]."

Or:

"Rewrite the following draft in my voice. Keep it emotionally warm and use metaphor where appropriate."

Step 3: Set the Tone Per Chapter or Section

Each chapter might have its own emotional flavor — even if the overall voice remains consistent.

Tone Prompt Examples:

"Write this section in a soft, reassuring tone."
"Make this sound more motivational and uplifting."
"Shift this paragraph to feel more intimate and reflective."
"Add playful language without sounding silly."

Step 4: Revise & Personalize

Even with a strong AI draft, you'll often want to:

- Add personal stories or examples
- Refine spiritual/philosophical language
- Adjust pacing (e.g., break up long paragraphs, add breath)

Prompt Tip:

"This sounds too generic. Rewrite with more heart and personal insight."

"Add three lines of poetic imagery that deepen the emotional resonance."

Use These Prompt Templates for Voice Alignment

- "Match the tone of this paragraph: [insert]. Now continue the chapter using the same voice."
- "Here's my outline. Write a first draft that reflects my brand: intuitive, wise, grounded, and transformative."
- "This section sounds flat. Can you rewrite it with more rhythm and emotional flow?"
- "Simplify this text, but keep the sacred and elevated tone."

Pro Tips to Keep Your Voice Strong

- Revisit your **"Voice Primer"** frequently in longer writing sessions
- Save samples of your past writing to use as reference
- Don't be afraid to revise what ChatGPT gives you — your edits are what make it *true* to you
- When in doubt, read your work aloud. If it doesn't *sound* like you, it isn't quite there yet

"Your voice is your signature. AI can echo it — but only you can originate it."

Giving ChatGPT Context: Setting the Scene

Help AI Understand What You're Writing So It Can Help You Write It Better

ChatGPT is powerful — but it's not psychic.
It doesn't know what you've already written. It doesn't remember your last book. It can't intuit your intention… unless you tell it.

That's why giving **context** is one of the most important — and most overlooked — steps in co-writing with AI.

When you set the scene clearly, ChatGPT can give you focused, relevant, and emotionally aligned responses that reflect your voice, vision, and goals.

WHY CONTEXT MATTERS

Without context, ChatGPT will:

- Make vague assumptions
- Default to generic phrasing
- Miss your tone or theme
- Misunderstand your intended audience

With context, it becomes a smart, insightful collaborator that can:

- Build directly on your past writing
- Mirror your narrative flow
- Offer tailored suggestions that *feel right*

What to Include When Giving Context

The more you include *up front*, the less editing you'll need *later*.

Here's what to tell ChatGPT:

1. **Your Role:** Who are you as the author?
2. **Your Audience:** Who are you speaking to?
3. **Your Purpose:** What are you trying to convey or achieve in this chapter or section?
4. **The Book So Far:** What has already been said or established?
5. **Scene/Chapter Details:** What's happening right now? What tone or energy should this carry?

Example Prompt With Strong Context:

"I'm writing a nonfiction book for intuitive entrepreneurs about using energy alignment in business. I'm on Chapter 4, which focuses on trusting intuitive nudges during decision-making. The tone is warm, empowering, and a little mystical. The reader has already learned the basics of energy awareness. Can you help me write the opening of this chapter with a metaphor about lighthouses and inner knowing?"

This provides:

- **Clarity of audience and theme**
- **Placement within the book**
- **Desired tone and direction**
- **Symbolic anchor for depth**

Layered Prompt Tip: You Can Add Context As You Go

If you forget to give full context at first, you can add it in follow-up prompts:

"Actually, in the previous chapter, I introduced the concept of energetic misalignment. Can you revise this section to feel like a natural continuation of that idea?"

"Here's a paragraph I wrote. Use it as context for the next section: [insert]."

Context Prompt Template

Use this any time you're starting a new scene, chapter, or concept:

"I'm writing a [genre] book for [audience]. This is for Chapter [#], which is about [main point]. The tone should be [tone], and the reader has already learned [what they know]. Can you help me write [specific part]?"

Pro Tips for Clearer Context

- Use bullet points if you're giving ChatGPT a lot of background
- Create a short "context intro" for your book and reuse it at the beginning of sessions
- If you're writing fiction, describe your character's mood, setting, and inner conflict in your prompt
- Keep a saved prompt template you can fill in quickly to start each new writing session

"When you give AI a compass, it doesn't wander — it navigates. Your context becomes the map to your message."

Writing Dialogue, Descriptions, and Internal Monologue

Bringing Your Story to Life With Emotional Depth and Detail

Whether you're writing fiction or creative nonfiction, the elements that breathe life into your chapters are **dialogue, sensory description, and internal reflection.** These are the threads that let your readers *feel* the story — not just read it.

ChatGPT can help you shape, enhance, or even generate these elements from scratch. But the results only shine when you guide it with clear character intention, emotional tone, and desired rhythm.

Writing Dialogue with ChatGPT

Dialogue isn't just people talking — it reveals:

- Character dynamics
- Conflict or tension
- Inner beliefs and unspoken fears
- Plot movement in real-time

Prompt Example:

"Write a conversation between a skeptical FBI agent and a woman who claims she receives messages from angels. Keep the tension subtle but emotionally charged."

Tips for Better Dialogue Prompts:

- Set the scene: Where are they? What just happened?
- Clarify tone: Is it playful, heated, sarcastic, vulnerable?
- Add emotional subtext: What is unsaid but *felt*?

Follow-Up Prompts:

"Make this dialogue more natural and emotionally layered."
"Add subtle tension between the characters without making them argue."
"Shorten this to sound more realistic and less formal."

Writing Vivid Descriptions with ChatGPT

Descriptions should evoke atmosphere, emotion, and world-building — without overwhelming the reader.

Prompt Example:

"Describe a healing temple hidden in a misty mountain forest. Use poetic language, rich sensory detail, and a mystical tone."

Ask ChatGPT to:

- Focus on a specific sense (sound, scent, texture)
- Reflect a character's emotions through the environment
- Vary pacing with long lyrical lines or short, punchy imagery

Advanced Prompt:

"Describe the main character's childhood bedroom in a way that hints at both comfort and grief. Make the space feel emotionally symbolic."

Crafting Internal Monologue and Emotional Reflection

Internal thoughts add depth, reveal motivation, and create intimacy between reader and character — especially in first-person or close third-person writing.

Prompt Example:

"Write a short internal monologue for a woman who just discovered her grandmother's journal, which reveals a family secret about intuitive healing."

Use ChatGPT to:

- Explore emotional undercurrents
- Reveal hesitation, self-doubt, or breakthroughs
- Reflect on spiritual or philosophical meaning

Follow-Up Prompts:

"Make this more emotionally conflicted — she feels both wonder and betrayal."
"Add sensory language to show how this moment is affecting her body."

Combining All Three Elements in One Scene

Master Prompt Example:

"Write a scene where a character walks through a forgotten garden, remembers a painful childhood memory, and speaks briefly with a friend who helps her shift perspective. Include physical description, brief dialogue, and internal reflection. Tone: nostalgic, hopeful."

This creates layered content you can then edit, restructure, or rewrite — with your voice guiding the final result.

Editing with Precision

Use ChatGPT for refinement:

- "Make this monologue shorter and more poetic."
- "Add metaphors related to nature."
- "Rewrite this dialogue to match the character's nervous personality."

"When used with intention, AI doesn't just create words — it evokes experience. It helps you shape moments that stay with the reader long after the page is turned."

Nonfiction: Supporting Evidence, Quotes, and Data

Grounding Your Message in Credibility and Clarity

Great nonfiction isn't just inspiring — it's *trustworthy*.
Whether you're teaching, guiding, or persuading, readers want to know:
"Why should I believe you?"

Supporting your content with research, quotes, data, and expert insight builds that trust. While ChatGPT can't pull real-time citations, it *can* help you simulate, organize, and present supporting information clearly and effectively.

Let's explore how to use AI to enrich your nonfiction chapters with substance — without getting overwhelmed.

Clarifying What You Want to Support

Before you ask ChatGPT for help, identify what you're trying to strengthen:

- A **claim or concept**?
- A **step in your process**?
- A **myth you're debunking**?
- A **pattern you've observed** through experience?

Then ask:

"What kind of evidence would make this more credible — a quote, a stat, a case study, or a story?"

Simulating Data and Statistics

While ChatGPT doesn't access live databases, it can **simulate examples** or summarize known trends based on its training data.

Prompt Examples:

"Summarize the common signs of burnout in holistic practitioners using a confident but conversational tone."

"Give me an example statistic (fictional but realistic) about the rise in energy healing businesses over the past decade."

"Write a paragraph explaining the impact of emotional trauma on physical health, using a calm, evidence-based tone."

Important: Always fact-check any data or stats before publishing. AI-generated numbers are *not verified*.

Adding Famous Quotes, Sayings, or Wisdom

ChatGPT can recall many widely-known quotes, proverbs, or teachings that add weight or beauty to your writing.

Prompt Examples:

"Give me 3 quotes from well-known thought leaders about intuition or inner knowing."

"Find short quotes that reflect the importance of emotional self-care from spiritual or wellness figures."

"Write a poetic sentence that sounds like it could come from Rumi or Kahlil Gibran — but make it original."

Pro Tip: Ask ChatGPT to paraphrase well-known ideas into your voice:

"Rewrite this quote in a style that fits my tone: [insert quote]."

Structuring Research-Based Content

If you're using case studies, historical background, or comparisons, ChatGPT can help you organize and simplify complex info.

Prompt Examples:

"Structure a section comparing traditional medicine and energy healing in a balanced, educational tone."

"Break down the chakra system into a chart for beginner readers, with color, element, and associated emotion."

Explaining Scientific or Spiritual Concepts

Sometimes you need to explain something nuanced in plain language. This is where ChatGPT really shines.

Prompt Examples:

"Explain quantum entanglement in simple language for a reader who's never studied physics."

"Describe how the nervous system responds to chronic stress using both medical and energetic perspectives."

You can even ask it to do multiple tone variations:

"Now rewrite it as if you're explaining it to a teenager."
"Make it more poetic or metaphorical without losing accuracy."

Building Credibility Brick by Brick

For every claim, you can prompt:

- "What's the energetic/spiritual explanation for this?"
- "What's the psychological/clinical view on this same issue?"
- "What's a real-life example or case study that illustrates this?"

This gives you **multiple angles** to support one key message.

"Truth becomes transformative when it's grounded — not just in belief, but in lived experience, shared wisdom, and real-world evidence."

Module-by-Module

Using ChatGPT to Structure Your Nonfiction Book

Turn Your Big Idea Into a Clear Teaching Journey

If you're writing a nonfiction book — especially one that teaches, guides, or transforms — it's helpful to think in **modules**, not just chapters.

Modules are *teaching phases* or *core pillars* of your message. Within each module are **topics** — these can become individual chapters, sections, or even lessons in a future course or program.

ChatGPT can help you structure your entire book this way — all you have to do is know **how to ask.**

Step 1: Tell ChatGPT What Your Book Is About

Be clear about your concept, audience, and goal.

Prompt Example:

"I want to write a nonfiction book for [audience] about [topic]. The goal is to help them [transformation or result]. Can you suggest a 5- or 6-module structure for the book, with 3–5 topics in each module?"

This gives ChatGPT enough context to begin mapping your message into a step-by-step format.

Step 2: Refine the Structure

Once ChatGPT gives you a basic structure, you can guide it further:

Prompt Examples:

- "Make the module titles more action-oriented or emotionally resonant."
- "Can you revise the topics to sound more spiritual/informal/educational?"
- "Turn this into a course structure with lesson outcomes."
- "Match the tone of a self-help book for women over 40."

Step 3: Ask Follow-Up Questions for Depth

After you've chosen your modules and topics, go deeper:

"Now expand each topic into a short paragraph that explains what it covers."
"Suggest a journal prompt, exercise, or case study that could go with each topic."
"Which topics could become standalone blog posts or mini-workshops?"

Prompt Formula: Teach ChatGPT to Think Like a Teacher

Here's a powerful prompt you can copy and reuse:

"I'm writing a [nonfiction/self-help/spiritual/business] book for [target reader]. My topic is [brief description]. I want to organize the book like a teaching journey, with 5–6 core modules. Each module should contain 3–5 topics. Can you help me create this structure in a way that builds step-by-step and feels transformational for the reader?"

Optional Add-Ons to Ask For:

- Suggested **chapter titles**
- Emotional or spiritual **themes for each module**
- **Quotes**, stories, or metaphors to open each topic
- Reflection questions to include at the end of each chapter

"When you structure your book in modules, you're not just writing — you're teaching. You're creating a clear path that transforms your reader's life, one step at a time."

How to Ask ChatGPT for Modules and Topics (Nonfiction Book Structure)

Use These Exact Prompts to Build and Teach Your Book

STEP 1: Ask for the Book Structure (Modules + Topics)

Use this exact prompt to get your outline started:

"I am going to write a book about [insert your book topic or concept]. Give me the modules and topics I should include. Add anything you think is important and relevant for this subject."

You can also clarify:

- Who your audience is (beginner? practitioner?)
- What kind of tone you want (professional? warm? spiritual?)
- Whether the book should follow a transformational arc, step-by-step learning model, or practical application

EXAMPLE PROMPT:

I am going to write a book about energy healing and trauma release. Give me the modules and topics I should include. Add anything you think is important and relevant for this subject.

ChatGPT will then reply with a structured breakdown like:

- **Module 1: Foundations of Energy Healing**
  - What Is Energy Healing?
  - The Aura, Chakras, and Energy Fields
  - Safety, Ethics, and Practitioner Preparation

...and so on.

STEP 2: Ask to Expand One Topic at a Time

Once you receive your structure, you now deepen each topic by asking ChatGPT to teach it back to you — as if you were a new student.

"Tell me all about [insert topic] as if I were a student who knew nothing about it. Be clear, thorough, and use examples or metaphors where helpful. Keep the tone [educational/warm/engaging/informal, etc.]."

EXAMPLE PROMPT:

Tell me all about "The Aura, Chakras, and Energy Fields" as if I were a student who knew nothing about it. Be clear and thorough. Use examples and keep the tone gentle and educational.

To carry on with the next topic:

- Now for, _____
- Now, all about _____

Bonus Follow-Up Prompts to Go Deeper on Any Topic

Once you've expanded the topic, you can ask:

- "Give me a real-world example or case study that demonstrates this."
- "Suggest a journal reflection or exercise to include after this section."
- "What are common misconceptions people have about this?"
- "Can you summarize this in a diagram or table format for visual learners?"

"This is how you co-write a book —
not by asking for everything at once,
but by building it piece by piece.
You are the guide, and ChatGPT is
your assistant — always ready to
expand, clarify, or support your next
idea."

Writing Exercises & Prompts

Using ChatGPT to Create Reflection, Engagement, and Action in Your Book

Writing a book isn't just about what *you* say — it's about what your reader *experiences*. Especially in nonfiction, **writing exercises and prompts** help your reader process the information, apply it to their life, and move from insight into transformation.

Whether you're writing a self-help book, a teaching guide, or a spiritual journey, you can use ChatGPT to generate meaningful, on-topic activities that deepen learning and connection.

WHY USE WRITING EXERCISES IN YOUR BOOK?

- They turn passive reading into **active engagement**
- They help readers **process emotions, memories, or beliefs**
- They support **integration and real-life application**
- They create **moments of clarity and self-discovery**
- They make your book **more interactive, useful, and valuable**

How to Prompt ChatGPT to Create Custom Writing Prompts

Start with a clear request like:

"Create 5 reflective writing prompts for a chapter about [topic]. They should help the reader explore [emotion/theme/transformation]."

Prompt Examples:

"Give me 5 journaling prompts to follow a chapter on self-trust and intuition."

"Create writing exercises that help the reader reflect on energy blocks in their body."

"Suggest end-of-chapter prompts that support goal setting after reading about burnout recovery."

"I'm writing for heart-centered entrepreneurs. Give me prompts that connect their business goals with their deeper purpose."

Types of Exercises ChatGPT Can Generate

1. **Reflective Prompts**

"What beliefs are you ready to release around [topic]?"
"When was the last time you felt fully aligned — and what led you there?"

2. **Goal-Oriented Prompts**

"Write a vision statement for your next chapter in life or business."
"List 3 micro-changes you can make this week to embody this chapter's lesson."

3. **Visualization or Embodiment Prompts**

"Close your eyes and imagine your healed self. What do you feel, see, hear?"
"Describe the color, shape, and sensation of your inner resistance."

4. **Creative Exploration Prompts**

"Write a letter to your future self from your higher self."
"Tell a short story where you are the guide you always needed."

5. **Spiritual or Energetic Prompts**

"What chakra feels most activated right now — and what might it be asking you to notice?"
"Tune into your body. What word or image surfaces? Free-write on that for 5 minutes."

Ask ChatGPT to Match Tone & Depth

You can guide the voice and energy of the prompts with instructions like:

- "Make them gentle and encouraging, ideal for emotional healing."
- "Use poetic language that evokes inner clarity."
- "Keep the language simple for beginners in spiritual work."
- "Sound like a teacher guiding a classroom, but with warmth and humor."

Prompt Templates to Keep Reusing

"Give me 3 writing prompts for [chapter topic] that focus on [emotion/goal/audience experience]."

"What's a writing exercise I could include that helps the reader apply [lesson] to their real life?"

"Create a reflection journal entry based on this chapter's takeaway."

"Books that invite action don't just teach — they transform. When you ask the reader to write with you, you give them space to write their own story inside yours."

CHAPTER 4: Rewriting and Refining

Asking ChatGPT for Rewrites or Style Adjustments

Refine, Rework, and Elevate Your Writing Without Losing Your Voice

Sometimes your first draft is close — but not quite.
Maybe it's too wordy. Too stiff. Not emotional enough. Or it just doesn't *sound like you.* That's where ChatGPT becomes a powerful editing partner.

Rather than rewriting from scratch, you can guide ChatGPT to **adjust tone, style, structure, or rhythm** — while preserving your message.

This section shows you exactly how to ask for the right kind of rewrite, whether you want your text to sound softer, stronger, funnier, deeper, or simply more *you.*

Common Reasons Authors Request Rewrites

- The tone is off (too formal, too vague, too robotic)
- The message is clear, but the emotion isn't there
- Sentences are too long, repetitive, or clunky
- You want the writing to sound more personal, warm, or poetic

- You're trying to match a specific voice (your own or your brand's)

Basic Rewrite Prompt Example

"Rewrite this paragraph to sound more conversational and engaging, like I'm speaking directly to the reader."

Or:

"Make this section more emotionally impactful, while keeping the message the same."

Just paste your text underneath and let ChatGPT do the rest.

Common Style Adjustments to Request

Here are phrases you can use in your prompts to get very specific results:

- "Make this more poetic and soulful."
- "Shorten and simplify this for clarity."
- "Add metaphors or sensory language."
- "Make it sound like Brené Brown meets Deepak Chopra."
- "Rewrite with a confident, mentor-style voice."
- "Turn this into bullet points or a list format."
- "Make it more professional and polished."
- "Soften the tone and add empathy."
- "Add curiosity or surprise to the introduction."
- "Use a storytelling tone instead of a factual tone."

Layered Rewrite Flow: Step-by-Step Editing with AI

Instead of one big revision, try asking ChatGPT to refine in stages:

1. **"Here's my draft. First, fix grammar, clarity, and flow."**
2. **"Now rewrite it in a warm, grounded tone."**
3. **"Add a metaphor about transformation or healing."**
4. **"Can you make the rhythm feel more lyrical or inspirational?"**

This process gives you control while letting ChatGPT do the heavy lifting.

Advanced Prompt Example

"I wrote this passage for a chapter on self-sabotage. It's technically fine, but it lacks emotional depth. Can you rewrite it so it speaks directly to the reader's pain and includes a metaphor about being stuck in a maze? Keep the tone encouraging and insightful."

This kind of input gives ChatGPT exactly what it needs to *transform your content* — not just tweak it.

Also Try These Rewrite Prompts

- "What's missing in this paragraph emotionally?"
- "Make this sound like it's part of a spiritual self-help book."
- "Polish this into something I could confidently publish."
- "Help me simplify this for a 6th-grade reading level without losing depth."
- "Make this stronger without sounding aggressive."
- "Rewrite this with gentle humor."
- "Inject a little more rhythm and flow — like spoken word."

"You don't need to throw away your first draft. You just need the right words to help it shine. And often, the magic is already there — it just needs to be spoken in your truest voice."

Getting Feedback on Flow, Tone, and Clarity

Let AI Act as Your First Beta Reader — Honest, Fast, and Judgment-Free

You've written your draft — now it's time to find out:

- Does it *flow* well?
- Is the *tone* consistent with your message and audience?
- Are your ideas *clear* and easy to follow?

Before asking a human editor, ChatGPT can serve as your **first-pass reader** — giving structured feedback on how your writing feels, reads, and lands.

THE KEY? ASK THE RIGHT QUESTIONS.

Why Use ChatGPT for Editorial Feedback?

- Instant insight, without waiting on a human beta reader
- Honest but neutral — no ego, no sugarcoating
- Focused on improvement, not just correction
- Helps you catch issues before hiring a professional editor
- You can ask it for feedback again and again — for free

How to Prompt for Feedback on Your Writing

Paste your passage, then ask:

"Can you give me feedback on this excerpt? I want to know if it flows well, if the tone is appropriate for [audience or genre], and whether anything is unclear or confusing."

You can add:

"Please highlight sentences that feel awkward, repetitive, or overly formal."

Prompt Examples for Specific Feedback Needs

- "Does this introduction feel engaging and clear to a beginner?"
- "Is the tone of this paragraph warm and encouraging?"
- "Does this chapter flow logically, or does it jump around too much?"
- "Can you simplify or restructure any areas that feel clunky?"
- "I'm going for a calm, reflective tone — does this match that?"
- "What suggestions do you have to improve clarity and rhythm?"

What Kind of Feedback Can ChatGPT Give?

1. **Flow Feedback**

Helps you spot pacing issues, abrupt transitions, or sentence structure problems

2. **Tone Feedback**

Tells you if the writing feels too formal, too casual, too cold, or inconsistent

3. **Clarity Feedback**

Highlights over-complicated wording, vague concepts, or missing explanations

4. **Audience Alignment**

Can evaluate if your message matches the needs and language level of your reader (beginner, advanced, niche, general)

Refine with Follow-Up Prompts

Once you get feedback, use these to improve:

"Thanks! Can you rewrite this with better flow but keep the tone the same?"
"Can you give me alternative wordings for the clunky parts you identified?"
"Now rewrite this so it's easier to understand, but keep the message intact."
"Help me restructure this to make the logic more sequential."

Example Prompt Flow

"Here's my chapter introduction. I want it to feel calm, wise, and inspiring. Can you give feedback on tone, and let me know if the message is clear to someone new to energy healing?"

ChatGPT returns with suggestions and highlights issues in flow, sentence rhythm, or missed clarity.
→ You follow up:

"Can you revise it for smoother transitions and more vivid language?"

Now your paragraph *sings*.

"Great writing isn't just about what you say — it's about how your reader receives it. ChatGPT can help you tune into that unseen connection, sentence by sentence."

Improving Character Development or Argument Strength

Deepen Fictional Characters — or Fortify Nonfiction Logic — with the Right Prompts

Whether you're writing a gripping novel or a powerful nonfiction book, your message hinges on one of two things:

- In **fiction**, your reader needs **characters they care about** — with motives, flaws, and arcs they can emotionally invest in.
- In **nonfiction**, your reader needs a **clear, strong argument** — backed by evidence, logic, and emotional resonance.

ChatGPT can help you enhance **both** — if you know how to guide it.

CHARACTER DEVELOPMENT IN FICTION

Shallow characters lose readers. Rich characters keep them turning pages. Ask ChatGPT to:

- Flesh out backstory, motivations, inner conflicts
- Build character arcs that feel earned and realistic
- Add emotional texture, growth, and flaws
- Identify inconsistencies in behavior or dialogue
- Reveal what your character *wants* vs. what they *need*

Prompts for Developing Characters:

"This is my main character: [brief description]. Help me deepen their internal conflict and give them a more layered backstory."

"What fears, flaws, and hidden desires might someone like this have?"

"Can you map a believable character arc that takes them from [starting point] to [ending point] over 10 chapters?"

"Suggest ways I can show, not tell, that this character is afraid of abandonment."

"Help me revise this scene to make the character's reaction feel more emotionally grounded."

Tip: Ask ChatGPT to Play the Character

Use this immersive prompt:

"Pretend you are [character's name]. Tell me in your own words what you're afraid of and what you really want."

This unlocks emotional insight you might not have considered.

Argument Strength in Nonfiction

In nonfiction, weak arguments = lost trust. Whether you're persuading, informing, or teaching, you want ideas that:

- Follow a logical path
- Are backed by data, analogies, or personal stories
- Address objections or common questions
- Connect emotionally as well as intellectually

Prompts for Strengthening Arguments:

"This is my main idea: [insert idea]. Help me build a stronger supporting case with logic and examples."

"What counterarguments might readers have, and how can I address them respectfully?"

"What evidence or stories would strengthen this point?"

"Can you rewrite this paragraph to sound more persuasive and authoritative?"

"Does this argument follow a logical flow, or is anything missing?"

Use ChatGPT to Stress-Test Your Ideas

Ask:

"If you disagreed with this idea, what would you say? Now help me write a response to that objection."

"What real-life examples, case studies, or research would support this claim?"

This turns your chapter into a well-reasoned conversation — not just a monologue.

"Characters are the soul of fiction. Logic is the spine of nonfiction. In either case, ChatGPT helps you go deeper — until your story or message is no longer just written… it's felt."

Removing Redundancies or Awkward Phrasing

Make Your Writing Clearer, Smoother, and More Professional

Even the best writers repeat themselves. Or over-explain. Or use phrasing that *almost* works — but lands flat. The good news? ChatGPT is exceptional at spotting:

- Repetitive wording
- Clunky sentence structure
- Awkward transitions or filler phrases
- Overuse of certain words
- Passive voice that weakens your message

This section will show you how to prompt ChatGPT to **tighten your prose** and make it shine — without stripping away your voice.

WHY ELIMINATE REDUNDANCIES AND AWKWARD PHRASING?

- Improves **readability and flow**
- Keeps the reader **engaged and moving forward**
- Adds **professional polish** to your writing
- Reduces **mental friction** for your audience
- Makes your ideas **easier to understand and retain**

Prompt Examples to Remove Repetition and Clutter

"Please edit this paragraph to remove redundancies and awkward phrasing, while keeping the tone intact."

"Tighten this text — make it clearer and more concise."

"Can you eliminate unnecessary repetition and improve sentence rhythm?"

"Revise this section for clarity, and point out any phrases that feel unnatural or overly formal."

Common Redundancies to Watch For (and Ask ChatGPT to Fix)

- "Absolutely essential" → Just "essential"
- "Past history" → Just "history"
- "Each and every" → One or the other
- "In my personal opinion" → Just "in my opinion"
- "End result" → Just "result"

You can paste your full chapter and ask:

"Highlight any phrases that are redundant or repetitive and suggest cleaner alternatives."

Advanced Clean-Up Prompt

"Here's a chapter draft. Please do a line edit focused on conciseness and clarity. Fix redundancies, awkward transitions, and filler words — but keep the tone conversational and engaging."

Want more precision? Add your style:

"Keep the voice warm and reflective — like a trusted guide, not a corporate writer."

Optional: Ask for a "Before and After" Comparison

Prompt:

"Can you show me the original version alongside your revised version so I can see what changed?"

This is excellent for learning how to improve your own writing over time.

Use ChatGPT as a Real-Time Clarity Coach

Ask:

"What parts of this sound unclear, bloated, or overly wordy?"
"Can you trim this without losing its meaning?"
"How would you say this more simply and powerfully?"
"Rewrite this in a way that flows better and gets to the point faster."

"Clean writing isn't just about saying less — it's about saying more with fewer words. ChatGPT helps you carve away the noise so your message shines through."

Editing Prompts:

"Make this more emotional..." / "Rewrite this in a stronger voice..."

Simple Prompts That Unlock Powerful Revisions

Some of the most transformative improvements in your writing happen when you ask ChatGPT to **go deeper** — to amplify the emotion, sharpen the voice, or elevate the impact of your words.

This section shows how to use **short, powerful editing prompts** to instantly upgrade your writing. These requests don't require lengthy instructions — just clear intention.

TONE AND VOICE ARE EVERYTHING

Voice is how your writing *feels*.
Tone is how your writing *sounds*.
ChatGPT can adjust both with just a sentence of direction.

Whether you want **gentle, bold, humorous, heartfelt, reflective**, or **commanding**, your prompt sets the stage.

Prompt Examples to Enhance Emotion and Impact

These are plug-and-play prompts you can use with any paragraph, chapter, or section:

"Make this more emotional and heartfelt."
"Rewrite this to sound bolder and more confident."
"Can you deepen the emotional intensity without being dramatic?"
"Soften this to feel more nurturing and supportive."
"Add warmth and vulnerability to this passage."
"Rewrite with a sense of urgency or conviction."

"Give this a poetic, lyrical tone."
"Make this sound like it's coming from a wise mentor."
"Turn this into an inspirational call to action."

Prompt + Sample Text = Quick Transformation

Prompt:

"Make this more emotional and personal."
Sample Text:
"Sometimes, change is necessary for growth."

AI Revision:

"There are moments when life whispers — or shouts — that it's time to let go, to grow into who you were always meant to be. It hurts, but it heals."

This is the power of one well-phrased request.

Prompt Stack: Layered Refinement

Use prompts in a sequence for richer results:

1. **"Polish this paragraph for clarity and flow."**
2. **"Now add emotional depth and personal insight."**
3. **"Finally, infuse it with a sense of hope and empowerment."**

The result: clean, compelling, and deeply felt writing — *in your voice.*

Prompts to Experiment With Based on Your Genre

For Fiction:

"Add tension and emotional stakes."
"Deepen the character's emotional response here."
"Rewrite this moment to evoke heartbreak/regret/longing."

For Nonfiction:

"Strengthen the call to action."
"Make this advice feel more personal and encouraging."
"Give this example more emotional weight."

For Memoir:

"Bring the memory to life with sensory detail and emotion."
"Make this reflection more raw and honest."
"Soften this memory without losing the pain."

Pro Tip: Ask ChatGPT Why It Changed Something

Prompt:

"Explain what you changed and why, so I can learn to do it myself."

This trains your editorial eye while letting ChatGPT serve as a mentor.

"Sometimes, one line is all it takes to turn good writing into unforgettable writing. The key is knowing how to ask for it."

CHAPTER 5: Essential Book Sections

How to Prompt for: Title Brainstorming

Generate Titles That Grab Attention, Capture Essence, and Sell Your Book

A great title isn't just a label — it's a **promise to the reader.** It communicates genre, tone, subject, and benefit in just a few words. Whether you're writing a self-help guide, a romantic novel, or a children's adventure, your title can make or break that first impression.

The good news? ChatGPT is excellent at brainstorming title options — **as long as you guide it well.**

BEFORE YOU PROMPT: GATHER YOUR ESSENTIALS

To get the best title suggestions, give ChatGPT:

- Your **book's topic or concept**
- The **target audience**
- The **desired tone** (e.g., playful, dramatic, spiritual, practical)
- A **one-line description** or elevator pitch (if you have one)
- **Comparable book titles** you admire (optional but helpful)

Prompt Formula: Title Brainstorming

"Can you give me 10 title ideas for a [genre] book about [main idea or transformation], written for [audience], with a [tone] style?"

Example:

"Can you give me 10 title ideas for a nonfiction book about using ChatGPT to help authors write and publish their books? It's for new and experienced writers, and the tone is inspiring, practical, and a little tech-savvy."

Other Title Prompt Variations

- **"Give me book title ideas that sound like bestsellers in this genre."**
- **"Can you make the titles more poetic?"**
- **"Try again with a more mystical/spiritual/businesslike edge."**
- **"Now give me some two-word or three-word titles only."**
- **"Which of these titles sounds most marketable to a wellness audience?"**
- **"Give me pun-based titles or clever wordplay for this book idea."**

Tips for Getting Better Results

- **Be specific about what you want.** A "spiritual empowerment book for women in midlife" gives more direction than "a personal growth book."
- **Ask for subtitle suggestions, too.** Many books sell on subtitle clarity (especially in nonfiction).
- **Ask ChatGPT to explain its reasoning.**

"Why do you think this title works best for my topic?"

Subtitle Prompt Example

"Now give me subtitle options for this book that highlight the benefit/result the reader will gain."

You'll get responses like:

"Harnessing AI to Write Better, Faster, and Smarter"
"A Practical Guide for Writers Who Want to Partner with Technology"
"From Idea to Bestseller Using the Power of ChatGPT"

✅ Checklist for a Strong Title + Subtitle

- ✅ Easy to say and remember
- ✅ Clear genre or benefit
- ✅ Tone matches content
- ✅ Feels fresh but not confusing
- ✅ Invites curiosity or emotion
- ✅ Works well in a small image (thumbnail!)

"Titles are the soul of marketing in just a few words. Let ChatGPT help you find the one that opens the door to your reader's heart and curiosity."

How to Prompt for: Subtitle Suggestions

Clarify the Promise of Your Book — and Boost Its Market Appeal

If the **title** grabs attention, the **subtitle** explains *why* the reader should care.

In nonfiction especially, a subtitle plays a crucial role in:

- Highlighting the **transformation** or **benefit**
- Clarifying the **topic** and **audience**
- Conveying the **tone** and **value** of the book
- Boosting **SEO** and discoverability on search engines and platforms like Amazon

ChatGPT is excellent at brainstorming multiple subtitle variations once it understands your concept and goals.

PROMPT FORMULA: SUBTITLE BRAINSTORMING

"Here's my title: [insert title]. The book is about [topic or transformation], and it's for [audience]. Can you give me 10 subtitle suggestions that highlight the core benefit or purpose?"

Example:

"Here's my title: *How to Use ChatGPT for Authors*. The book teaches authors how to use ChatGPT to brainstorm, outline, write, and refine their books. It's for beginner to experienced writers. Can you give me subtitle ideas that are inspiring, practical, and clear?"

Prompt Variations to Use

- **"Make the subtitles sound benefit-driven and specific."**
- **"Can you rewrite these with more emotional pull?"**
- **"Try subtitle ideas that use numbers or power words."**
- **"Now give subtitle suggestions that sound professional and technical."**
- **"Give subtitle options that feel creative, witty, or thought-provoking."**

Pro Tip: Ask for Subtitle Types

You can specify the kind of subtitle you want. For example:

- **Transformational:**

"Unlocking Your Inner Author with AI-Enhanced Creativity"

- **Instructional:**

"A Step-by-Step Guide to Writing and Publishing with ChatGPT"

- **Inspirational:**

"Partnering with AI to Turn Imagination Into Published Reality"

- **SEO-Friendly:**

"Using AI Writing Tools to Brainstorm, Draft, and Sell Your Book"

Use This Follow-Up Prompt to Refine

"Can you rank these by strongest emotional appeal?"
"Which one would perform best in Amazon search results

and why?"
"Combine these two ideas into a single subtitle."

☑ Checklist: What Makes a Great Subtitle

- ☑ Explains **what** the book is about
- ☑ Hints at **who** it's for
- ☑ Highlights a **benefit or transformation**
- ☑ Evokes the **tone** of the book
- ☑ Stays under **12–14 words** if possible
- ☑ Works well paired with the main title

"A good title sparks interest. A great subtitle seals the deal."

How to Prompt for: Dedication

Craft a Personal, Meaningful Dedication That Resonates

A book dedication is often short—but powerful. It gives you a chance to:

- Honor someone meaningful in your life
- Share a quiet personal moment with your readers
- Set the emotional tone for the journey ahead

Whether heartfelt, humorous, or poetic, a good dedication feels authentic. ChatGPT can help you craft it—especially if you're unsure how to express your intention in just a few lines.

PROMPT FORMULA: CREATING A DEDICATION

"Help me write a dedication for this book. It's about [brief description of the book], and I'd like to dedicate it to [person, group, or idea], because [reason why]. Please offer a few tone options: heartfelt, poetic, and concise."

Example:

"Help me write a dedication for my book *How to Use ChatGPT for Authors*. I want to dedicate it to all the writers who were once too afraid to start. Give me three versions: one simple, one inspirational, and one poetic."

Prompt Variations to Try

- **"Make it humorous but sincere."**
- **"Can you make it sound like it's to the reader, not a person I know?"**

- **"Dedicate this to my late mentor, with a tone of deep respect."**
- **"Can you make this dedication double as a subtle message to aspiring creatives?"**

Example Outputs

Heartfelt:

To every writer who's whispered, "I don't know where to start." This is for you.

Poetic:

For the quiet creators, the midnight dreamers, and the voices waiting to be heard.

Simple:

Dedicated to my family, who always believed in the power of my words—even when I didn't.

☑ Checklist: A Great Dedication

- ☑ Is **short** (1–3 lines)
- ☑ Feels **genuine and personal**
- ☑ Matches your **tone** (inspirational, tender, funny, bold)
- ☑ Doesn't need to explain—just **honor or thank**

You Can Also Ask ChatGPT to Help Refine It

Prompt:

"Here's my draft dedication: [paste it]. Can you improve the tone and polish the wording while keeping my intention?"

"A dedication isn't just who it's to—
it's what you're standing for."

How to Prompt for: Acknowledgments

Gratitude in Print – Honoring Those Who Helped You Along the Way

The acknowledgments section is where you **step out of the narrative** and personally thank the people, organizations, and energies that supported your book's creation. It can be emotional, professional, or a blend of both.

With the right prompt, ChatGPT can help you organize your thoughts, polish your message, and create a meaningful and structured acknowledgment section—without sounding cliché or forced.

PROMPT FORMULA: WRITING ACKNOWLEDGMENTS

"Help me write the acknowledgments for my book. I want to thank [list of names, roles, or groups], and I'd like it to sound [tone: heartfelt, professional, casual, funny, poetic, etc.]."

Example:

"I want to thank my editor, beta readers, my partner, and the AI technology that helped bring this book to life. Please write this in a warm, sincere tone, with a touch of inspiration for other creatives."

Prompt Variations to Try

- **"Make this sound personal and not overly formal."**
- **"Help me structure this in paragraphs rather than a list."**
- **"Write this in my voice—conversational and grateful."**

- **"Include a final line that thanks the reader directly for joining me on this journey."**
- **"Can you break this into professional vs. personal thanks?"**

Sample Output Variations

Professional:

I'm deeply grateful to my editor, [Name], for their keen eye and unwavering support. To the early readers and reviewers who offered thoughtful feedback— thank you for helping shape this book. And to the OpenAI team, whose innovation made this writing partnership possible.

Heartfelt & Personal:

To my family, who never once asked why I needed one more writing session. To my partner, who believed in this project before I had words for it. And to every friend who cheered me on from the sidelines—your encouragement meant the world.

To the Reader (closing line):

And to you, dear reader—thank you for saying yes to this journey. May it inspire your own voice to rise.

✅ Checklist: Acknowledgment Tips

- ✅ Group similar people or roles together (e.g., professional, personal, inspiration)
- ✅ Mention people **by name** where appropriate
- ✅ Keep tone **genuine and balanced** (not overly long or self-indulgent)
- ✅ Consider **ending with a thank-you to the reader**

Refinement Prompt

"Here's a rough draft of my acknowledgments. Can you polish the language, fix the structure, and improve the flow while keeping my gratitude sincere?"
Paste your draft below.

"Acknowledging others isn't just courtesy — it's creative integrity. No book is written alone."

How to Prompt for: Author Bio

Crafting a Bio That Builds Trust, Connection, and Authority

Your author bio isn't just a summary of your career — it's an opportunity to:

- Establish your **credibility**
- Share your **personality**
- Connect with your **ideal reader**
- Encourage them to **follow you or explore more of your work**

Whether it appears in the back of your book, on Amazon, your website, or your media kit, ChatGPT can help you write a **compelling, polished, and authentic** bio.

PROMPT FORMULA: WRITING AN AUTHOR BIO

"Help me write an author bio for [name]. I've written a book about [topic], and my background includes [credentials, profession, personal experiences]. I want the tone to be [professional/friendly/inspirational/quirky/etc.], and it will be used on [Amazon/inside my book/my website/etc.]."

Example:

"Help me write an author bio for Dr. Constance Santego. She's the author of over 40 books on Reiki, natural healing, and intuition development. She is a Doctor of Natural Medicine, teacher, and international speaker. The tone should be inspiring and professional, with a hint of spiritual wisdom. This will be used inside the book and on the Amazon listing."

Prompt Variations to Use

- "Give me a short version (under 50 words)."
- "Now expand it to 150 words for Amazon and website."
- "Make this sound warmer and more personal."
- "Rewrite this with more focus on my mission."
- "Add a fun fact at the end to show personality."

Sample Output Formats

Short & Professional:

Dr. Constance Santego is a Doctor of Natural Medicine and the author of over 40 books on holistic wellness, Reiki, and spiritual transformation. Her mission is to empower others through healing, knowledge, and self-mastery.

Friendly & Inspiring (Medium):

Constance Santego is a healer, teacher, and prolific author whose books bridge the mystical and the practical. With over 25 years of experience in natural medicine, Reiki, and spiritual education, she guides readers on a path of intuitive awakening and holistic success. When she's not writing, you'll find her teaching, mentoring, or exploring energy medicine's newest frontiers.

With Personality (Extended):

Dr. Constance Santego is an author, educator, and Doctor of Natural Medicine dedicated to demystifying energy healing and spiritual development. With over 40 published works spanning fiction and nonfiction, she helps readers tap into their innate power through ancient wisdom and modern insight. Based in Canada, she spends her time writing, mentoring holistic practitioners, and occasionally wandering bookstores for inspiration (and strong coffee).

☑ Checklist: A Strong Author Bio Should…

- ☑ Include your **name and credentials** (if applicable)
- ☑ Summarize your **book's relevance** to your expertise
- ☑ Show a **bit of personality or mission**
- ☑ Fit the **platform or space** it's being used in
- ☑ Invite the reader to trust, relate, or explore more

Helpful Refinement Prompts

"Here's my current bio draft. Can you improve clarity, flow, and tone for my intended audience?"
"Rewrite this to sound more confident and visionary."
"Add a sentence that connects this bio to the theme of my current book."

"Your bio is more than your résumé — it's your invitation."

How to Prompt for: Preface vs. Foreword vs. Introduction

Understanding the Difference — and Knowing When to Use Each

These three sections often confuse new authors — and understandably so. While they can all appear at the beginning of a book, they serve very **different purposes**, are written by different people, and should be prompted differently when using ChatGPT.

Let's break down what each one is, when you need it, and how to ask ChatGPT to write it for you.

1. Preface

Purpose: The preface is written by the author. It explains **why you wrote the book, how it came to be,** or what inspired your journey.

Use it when:

- You want to share a personal backstory or intention
- You want to connect with the reader before the content begins
- The book required unique effort, research, or personal evolution

Prompt to Use:

"Help me write a preface for my book about [topic]. I want to share why I wrote it, how it came about, and what I hope readers gain from it. Make it sound [tone: honest/inspirational/spiritual/reflective]."

2. Foreword

Purpose: A foreword is written by **someone else**, not the author. Typically a well-known expert or respected figure in the field, it lends credibility and frames the book in context.

Use it when:

- You want to showcase third-party validation
- You have a mentor, influencer, or professional who supports your work
- Your book is part of a larger movement or field of study

Prompt to Use (if writing it yourself for someone to sign):

"Write a foreword for [Author Name]'s book on [topic], written by a respected [expert/mentor/professional]. Make it sound supportive, insightful, and like the author's work fills a gap in the field."

Prompt to send to someone else:

"Would you be willing to write a foreword for my book? I'd love you to share how you see this work helping others, and why you think this topic is important now."

3. Introduction

Purpose: The introduction helps the reader **understand what the book is about, how it's structured,** and **what they'll gain.**

Use it when:

- You want to orient the reader before Chapter One
- Your book has a clear method, system, or message
- You want to preview what's coming and how it will unfold

Prompt to Use:

"Write an introduction for my book on [topic]. It should explain what the book is about, who it's for, how it's organized, and what the reader will get from it. Use a clear and welcoming tone."

When to Include All Three

You *can* include all three, especially in nonfiction or professional books. Here's a simple layout:

1. **Foreword** (written by a guest expert)
2. **Preface** (personal backstory from the author)
3. **Introduction** (guide to the reader on how to use the book)

But if you're self-publishing and don't have a foreword writer, it's perfectly fine to include just the preface and intro—or even combine them.

Quick Reference Summary

Section	Written By	Purpose	Include When...
Preface	Author	Personal story, motivation, background	You want to share the *why*
Foreword	Someone else	Praise, context, external credibility	You have an expert willing to endorse it
Introduction	Author	What's inside, who it's for, how to use it	You want to orient and prepare the reader

"The beginning of a book is where trust is built. Use your voice—or someone else's—to open the door."

How to Prompt for: Back Cover Description (Short & Long)

Hook the Reader. Highlight the Journey. Inspire the Buy.

Your back cover description is arguably one of the most important pieces of writing for your book's success. It's your **sales pitch** — the compelling bridge between a curious browser and a committed reader.

There are typically **two versions**:

- **Short Version** (for web listings, ads, metadata – under 250 characters)
- **Long Version** (for the physical back cover or Amazon description – around 100–200 words)

ChatGPT can help you draft both with clarity, emotional appeal, and genre-appropriate structure.

What Makes a Strong Back Cover Description

- Clearly states what the book is about
- Tells the reader why it matters
- Speaks to the ideal reader (and their needs or interests)
- Reflects the tone of the book (light, serious, spiritual, playful, etc.)
- Ends with a strong *call to action* or reason to read now

PROMPT FORMULA: BACK COVER – LONG VERSION

"Write a back cover description (100–200 words) for my book titled [title]. It's about [brief summary]. The tone should be [inspirational/practical/romantic/mysterious/etc.], and it's meant for [target audience]."

Example:

"Write a 150-word back cover for my nonfiction book *How to Use ChatGPT for Authors*. It teaches writers how to brainstorm, write, edit, and publish using ChatGPT. Tone should be friendly and empowering. It's for authors, coaches, and creatives who want to write faster and better using AI."

PROMPT FORMULA: BACK COVER – SHORT VERSION (METADATA/ONLINE LISTINGS)

"Now write a short back cover description (under 250 characters) for the same book that works for Amazon or metadata."

Example Output:

Unlock the power of AI to brainstorm, write, and publish your book with ease. A step-by-step guide for modern authors ready to write smarter, not harder.

Prompt Variations to Try

- "Make it more emotionally compelling."
- "Focus on the reader's transformation or benefit."
- "Use storytelling in the opening line to draw them in."
- "Add a final question or hook that leaves them curious."
- "Write it in the style of a bestselling back cover."
- "Now rewrite it as if it's for a highly spiritual audience."
- "Try a version that would resonate with first-time authors."

- "Make it sound like a cinematic book trailer in words."

Editing Prompt for Refinement

"Here's my current back cover copy. Can you improve the flow, increase the emotional impact, and help it sell more effectively?"

(Paste your version into ChatGPT for polishing.)

☑ Checklist: Great Back Cover Copy Should...

- ☑ Highlight the **what + why + who**
- ☑ Use **genre-appropriate tone**
- ☑ Contain **a strong first sentence**
- ☑ Be **clear, not clever** (unless cleverness serves clarity)
- ☑ End with a hook, invitation, or benefit

"If your title opens the door, your back cover should invite the reader to walk through it."

How to Prompt for: Chapter Summaries

Clarify, Structure, and Strengthen Your Book — One Chapter at a Time

Chapter summaries serve **multiple purposes** throughout the book development process. They help you:

- Stay clear on the **main point of each chapter**
- Ensure **logical flow** from beginning to end
- Create material for your **table of contents, workbook, course, or pitch**
- Easily extract content for **marketing copy, presentations**, or **publisher proposals**

Whether you're planning your book, reviewing a draft, or prepping to pitch, ChatGPT can help you create clear, concise, and compelling chapter summaries with the right prompts.

What Is a Chapter Summary?

A chapter summary is a **brief description** (usually 1–4 sentences) that explains what happens in the chapter (for fiction) or what the reader learns (for nonfiction). It can be written in your voice or in third-person, depending on where it will be used.

PROMPT FORMULA: CHAPTER SUMMARIES (NONFICTION)

"Help me write chapter summaries for my nonfiction book titled [title]. Here are the chapter titles: [list them]. The tone should be [educational/inspirational/clear/concise], and each summary should explain what the chapter teaches."

Example:

"Help me write short chapter summaries for my book *How to Use ChatGPT for Authors*. Here are the chapters: 1. Getting Started with ChatGPT, 2. Brainstorming Book Ideas, 3. Writing Fiction with AI, 4. Editing with Prompts, etc."

PROMPT FORMULA: CHAPTER SUMMARIES (FICTION)

"Help me write chapter summaries for my novel titled [title]. It's about [brief plot summary]. I'll paste the chapter outline or events below. Write each summary in a way that explains the key plot point or emotional development."

Optional Variation:

"Make the tone match the genre: [mysterious/romantic/hopeful/dark/funny/etc.]."

Prompt to Summarize an Individual Chapter

"Summarize this chapter in 3 sentences. Here's what it covers: [paste the key points, outline, or full text]."
OR
"Summarize Chapter 5 for nonfiction readers. This chapter teaches [main concept]. Make it sound empowering and clear."

Great Uses for Chapter Summaries

- Table of contents with context
- Nonfiction workbook or course companion
- Query letters and proposals for agents/publishers
- Audiobook structure
- Lead magnets and free previews
- Reader discussion guides or book clubs

☑ Checklist: Strong Chapter Summaries Should…

- ☑ Be **brief but informative**
- ☑ Clearly reflect **the purpose or event** of the chapter
- ☑ Match the **tone and audience** of the book
- ☑ Help the reader **see the arc or logic** of your content

Polishing Prompts

- "Make these summaries more benefit-focused for the reader."
- "Add a bit more emotion or story flow."
- "Rewrite in first-person to match a workbook style."
- "Make this sound like it belongs on a nonfiction course syllabus."

"Your chapter summaries are the scaffolding that holds the reader's journey. Build them wisely."

How to Prompt for: Pull Quotes

Highlight Key Insights. Create Visual Impact. Inspire the Reader.

Pull quotes (also called callouts or highlighted quotes) are short, impactful phrases or sentences extracted from your book's content and emphasized in a larger font or graphic design. They break up the page visually, reinforce core ideas, and draw attention to key messages.

You'll often see pull quotes:

- In nonfiction books (especially personal development or business)
- On sales pages, social media, and marketing materials
- In journals or workbooks
- As shareable graphics or Kindle highlights

What Makes a Good Pull Quote?

A strong pull quote is:

- Short and powerful (1–3 sentences max)
- Emotionally resonant or motivational
- Thought-provoking or perspective-shifting
- Reflective of your core message or insight
- Stands on its own (even out of context)

PROMPT FORMULA: CREATING PULL QUOTES

"Generate 10 pull quotes from this content that are inspiring, clear, and stand-alone. The tone should match my book, which is [friendly/spiritual/authoritative/instructional/etc.]. Here's

the content:"
[Paste chapter, section, or key ideas]

Example:

"Give me 10 pull quotes from my book *How to Use ChatGPT for Authors*. It teaches writers how to use AI to brainstorm, write, and publish. The tone is empowering and practical."

Prompt to Extract from Chapters

"Pull the most powerful, motivational, or quotable lines from Chapter 3. Make them short, emotionally resonant, and suitable for highlighting in a book layout or sharing online."

Or:

"I want a pull quote that captures the essence of this paragraph: [paste text]. Keep it under 25 words."

Where to Use Pull Quotes

- Inside your book layout (between sections or to emphasize big takeaways)
- On your sales page or book funnel
- As social media graphics
- As part of your journal/workbook or course materials
- In marketing materials or bonus content

☑ Checklist: Effective Pull Quotes

- ☑ Short, standalone, and clear
- ☑ Speaks to the heart or mind
- ☑ Can be highlighted, quoted, or shared
- ☑ Matches tone of your message
- ☑ Invites curiosity, reflection, or agreement

Refinement Prompts

- "Make this quote sound more empowering."
- "Shorten this quote so it fits on a graphic."
- "Rewrite this so it sounds more inspirational/spiritual/provocative."
- "Give me one bold, tweetable version."

"Pull quotes are more than decoration — they're windows into your wisdom."

How to Prompt for: Chapter Titles

Turn Your Outline Into a Magnetic Reading Experience

Chapter titles aren't just labels — they're opportunities. A great chapter title pulls your reader in, gives them a preview of the content, and keeps them turning the page. Whether you're writing nonfiction or fiction, chapter titles should match your tone, style, and purpose.

ChatGPT can help you turn generic headings into compelling, creative, and cohesive titles that enhance your book's impact.

What Makes a Great Chapter Title?

- Clearly signals what the chapter is about
- Sparks curiosity or emotion
- Matches the tone of your book (serious, playful, mystical, instructive, etc.)
- Guides the reader while staying memorable

PROMPT FORMULA: CREATING CHAPTER TITLES

"Help me write compelling chapter titles for my book titled [Book Title]. Here's my chapter outline: [List your chapters with brief descriptions]. The tone should be [inspirational, fun, academic, practical, etc.]. Please make each title engaging and relevant to its content."

Example:

"Help me write creative chapter titles for my book *How to Use ChatGPT for Authors*. Here are the chapters: 1. Brainstorming Your Book Idea, 2. Structuring by Genre, 3. Drafting with Prompts, 4. Editing with AI. Tone: friendly and empowering."

Prompt for Revising a Specific Title

"Here's my current chapter title: 'Getting Started with Writing.' Can you rewrite it to sound more engaging, while keeping it clear?"
OR
"Make this title sound more professional/inspirational/mystical."

Tone Variations You Can Request

- **Instructive:** *How to Begin with Confidence*
- **Emotional:** *When Doubt Meets Determination*
- **Creative:** *Taming the Blank Page*
- **Spiritual:** *The Whisper Behind the Words*
- **Academic:** *Chapter One: Authorial Preparation and Conceptualization*
- **Playful:** *Plot Twists & Prompt Tricks*

☑ Checklist: Great Chapter Titles Should…

- ☑ Reflect the chapter's message
- ☑ Speak directly to your target reader
- ☑ Be consistent in tone with the rest of the book
- ☑ Offer clarity or curiosity — ideally both
- ☑ Fit the layout and style of your book design

Follow-Up Refinement Prompts

- "Give me a version of this chapter title that sounds more poetic."
- "Make it sound like a hook for a spiritual audience."
- "Shorten this to fit better in a minimal design."
- "Rewrite all my chapter titles in a consistent theme."
- "Turn these into questions or power statements."

"Your chapter titles are the signposts of your book's journey. Make sure each one points to possibility."

CHAPTER 6: Special Sections for Fiction

Scene-by-Scene Plotting

From Big Idea to Detailed Story: Use AI to Plot Your Story Like a Pro

Scene-by-scene plotting breaks your story down into actionable moments — giving your narrative structure, pacing, and emotional rhythm. Whether you're writing a novel, memoir, or narrative nonfiction, scene mapping helps ensure that every moment moves the story forward.

With ChatGPT, you can take your high-level idea or outline and transform it into a sequence of scenes, each with a purpose, setting, character intention, and emotional beat.

What Is Scene-by-Scene Plotting?

Scene-by-scene plotting is the act of outlining **what happens, to whom, where**, and **why it matters** — for each distinct unit of your story.

Each scene should serve at least one of the following:

- Advance the plot
- Reveal character
- Introduce or resolve conflict
- Deepen the theme
- Shift the emotional stakes

PROMPT FORMULA: FULL SCENE MAP

"Help me create a scene-by-scene breakdown for a [genre] novel titled [title]. It's about [brief premise]. I want around [X] scenes. Make sure each scene includes the setting, character actions, emotional tone, and how it advances the plot."

Example:

"Create a scene-by-scene outline for a romantic suspense novel titled *Beneath the Vineyards*. The story follows a travel writer and a winemaker who uncover a family secret while falling in love. I want 20 scenes, each with emotional stakes and plot movement."

Prompt to Expand from Outline to Scenes

"Here's my chapter outline. Break each chapter into 2–4 scenes with setting, character goals, and main action."

"I have this character arc. Can you suggest scenes that show key turning points in this arc?"

"Write a detailed description of Scene 7. Setting: vineyard at night. Emotional tone: tense but intimate. Goal: reveal a secret."

Prompt for Genre-Specific Scene Planning

- "Give me 10 emotional beats for a love story."
- "Plot out key scenes for a mystery novel with a twist ending."
- "Help me design scenes for a memoir about healing after loss."
- "What are the must-have scenes in a hero's journey format?"
- "I'm writing a thriller. Help me alternate between tension and release across scenes."

☑ Checklist: A Well-Plotted Scene Includes…

- ☑ **Who** is in it (main POV or driving characters)
- ☑ **Where** it takes place (setting and sensory tone)
- ☑ **What happens** (external action or decision)
- ☑ **Why it matters** (emotionally or narratively)
- ☑ A **shift** — something changes by the end

Refinement Prompts to Try

- "Make this scene more emotionally charged."
- "Add sensory details to this scene."
- "Introduce a small twist or surprise."
- "Tighten the pacing but keep the emotional core."
- "Rewrite this as a cinematic opening scene."

"Scenes are where your story breathes. Plotting them with purpose turns pages into transformation."

Worldbuilding with AI

Design Immersive Worlds that Feel Real, Layered, and Alive

Whether you're writing **fantasy, science fiction, historical fiction,** or even richly textured **contemporary fiction,** worldbuilding sets the stage for your characters and story to thrive. A well-built world is more than just setting—it's a **living system** of culture, geography, politics, belief, and sensory detail.

ChatGPT can help you go beyond flat descriptions and create **cohesive, believable environments** that are consistent, rich, and engaging for readers.

Why Worldbuilding Matters

Your world influences:

- **Character behavior and beliefs**
- **Story conflict and plot possibilities**
- **Cultural norms and language**
- **Visual and emotional immersion**

Even in contemporary or memoir writing, crafting an authentic "world" means building **a sense of place and atmosphere** that the reader can step into.

PROMPT FORMULA: BUILD A FICTIONAL WORLD

"Help me build a fictional world for a [genre] novel titled [Title]. The tone is [mystical/gritty/hopeful/etc.]. The world should include geography, climate, key cities or regions, politics, culture, and any magical or technological systems."

Example:

"Create a fantasy world for *The Fireborn Healer*. It's a spiritual fantasy about a girl who channels elemental energy. Include cultures, elemental temples, political factions, and sacred rituals."

Layered Prompt Breakdown

You can also ask ChatGPT to develop worldbuilding in layers:

1. **Geography & Environment**

   "Describe the natural terrain, climate, and regions of this world."

2. **Culture & Religion**

   "What are the belief systems and rituals of this society?"

3. **Politics & Power**

   "Who holds power? How is the government or leadership structured?"

4. **Technology or Magic Systems**

   "Describe how [magic/tech] works. What are its limits and consequences?"

5. **Daily Life**

   "What do people eat, wear, do for fun, or fear in this world?"

6. **Conflict Triggers**

"What tensions or divisions exist in this world that affect the plot?"

Nonfiction Application

Even nonfiction writers can use worldbuilding techniques to:

- Set the scene in memoir or narrative nonfiction
- Bring historical eras to life
- Evoke workplace culture, school systems, or industry environments
- Create immersive metaphors for coaching, teaching, or self-help material

Prompt:
"Help me describe a vivid sense of place for my memoir chapter set in 1980s Vancouver. Include smells, weather, slang, and emotional tone."

☑ Checklist: Strong Worldbuilding Covers...

- ☑ **Physical environment** (terrain, climate, location names)
- ☑ **Social systems** (roles, norms, customs)
- ☑ **Power structures** (government, religion, hierarchy)
- ☑ **Conflict zones** (past wars, societal rifts, forbidden zones)
- ☑ **Everyday sensory life** (food, festivals, colors, sounds)
- ☑ **Unique twist** that makes your world different or symbolic

Refinement Prompts

- "Make this setting feel more mystical."
- "Give this city a darker tone with hidden corruption."
- "Describe the festival traditions of this coastal village."
- "What would a secret society in this world believe and protect?"
- "Add an underworld or hidden dimension to this world."

"Worldbuilding isn't about inventing a place—it's about crafting a truth your characters believe in."

Character Profiles (Major and Minor)

Build Deep, Believable Characters Using AI-Powered Insight

Creating compelling characters is the heart of great storytelling. Your characters—both major and minor—need depth, flaws, goals, and unique voices to keep your reader emotionally invested.

With the right prompts, ChatGPT can help you **develop layered character profiles** quickly and consistently, so every figure in your story feels alive and purposeful.

Why Character Profiles Matter

- Consistency: Avoid contradictions in personality or backstory
- Voice: Make dialogue sound distinct and natural
- Motivation: Drive plot with believable decisions
- Detail: Add depth even to supporting characters
- Arc Planning: Track emotional and narrative growth

PROMPT FORMULA: CREATE A MAJOR CHARACTER PROFILE

"Create a detailed character profile for my protagonist. This is a [genre] novel called [title]. The main character is [name], a [age]-year-old [occupation/role]. The story follows them as they [main journey/conflict]. Please include background, personality traits, strengths, flaws, internal conflict, key relationships, and how they grow."

Example:

"Create a character profile for Claire Bennett, a 34-year-old travel writer in my romance novel *Under the Okanagan Sun*. She's burned out and questioning her future when she meets Ethan, a winemaker, while writing a feature story. Include her emotional wounds, ambitions, and arc."

PROMPT FORMULA: MINOR CHARACTER PROFILES

"Create a brief but vivid profile for a supporting character. They should add flavor to the story and support or challenge the main character. Include personality, their role in the plot, and one memorable trait or quirk."

Example:

"I need a best friend character for my main heroine. She should be funny, grounded, and say the hard truths. Give me her backstory and how she supports the protagonist emotionally."

Extended Prompt Options

- "Create a love interest with opposing traits to the main character."
- "Give me a villain who believes they're doing the right thing."
- "Design a mentor figure who challenges the main character spiritually."
- "Invent three minor characters who represent different elements of the setting."

What to Include in a Strong Profile

Element	Description
Name	Reflects tone, culture, or symbolism
Age & Appearance	Visual cues, posture, dress style
Background	Key past experiences, education, family
Personality	Traits, values, habits, emotional type
Motivations	Internal and external goals
Flaws/Wounds	Vulnerabilities or blind spots
Voice	Word choices, tone, rhythm of speech
Relationships	Allies, enemies, family, lovers
Character Arc	How they change or what they resist

Refinement Prompts

- "Make this character more flawed but lovable."
- "Add cultural or regional detail to make them feel rooted in place."
- "Help me build a psychological profile for this antagonist."
- "What secret could this character be hiding?"
- "Write dialogue between these two characters to show their dynamic."

"Characters don't need to be perfect—they need to be real, and that starts with knowing them better than they know themselves."

POV Consistency

Maintain a Clear Narrative Voice Throughout Your Book

Point of view (POV) is the lens through which your reader experiences the story. Maintaining POV consistency is essential to build trust with your reader, avoid confusion, and ensure your scenes feel immersive and intentional. Whether you're writing in **first-person**, **third-person limited**, or experimenting with **multiple POVs**, ChatGPT can help you spot inconsistencies and stay true to the chosen perspective.

Why POV Matters

- Sets emotional and narrative distance
- Shapes how much the reader knows at any moment
- Builds structure for internal thoughts, biases, and tone
- Affects how dialogue and action are interpreted

Common POV Types

POV	Description	Example
First Person ("I")	Inside the character's head—intimate and emotional	"I never thought the vineyard would change me."
Third-Person Limited	Narrator closely follows one character's perspective	"Claire stared at the vines, unsure of what to write next."
Third-Person Omniscient	All-knowing narrator who dips into any character's mind	"Claire feared the silence. Ethan, meanwhile, plotted his words."

POV	Description	Example
Second Person ("**You**")	Rare; puts the reader in the story	"You run your fingers over the old journal, unsure what to believe."

PROMPT FORMULA: ENSURING POV CONSISTENCY

"Can you review this passage and make sure the point of view is consistent with third-person limited from [Character Name]'s perspective?"
OR
"Rewrite this paragraph to stay inside the main character's head. Remove anything the character wouldn't realistically know or think."

Example Prompt:

"Here's a scene written in third-person limited from Claire's perspective, but I think I accidentally slipped into omniscient. Can you revise it so we only know what Claire knows, feels, and observes?"

How ChatGPT Helps With POV

- Identifies **head-hopping** (jumping between characters' internal thoughts mid-scene)
- Suggests **adjustments** to keep narrative grounded in one character's perception
- Helps you choose and maintain the **right narrative distance** (close vs. distant third)
- Rewrites scenes in **alternative POVs** so you can compare impact

Prompt: Switch POV for Style Testing

"Rewrite this scene from third-person to first-person to explore emotional intimacy."
"Can you show me how this scene would feel from the antagonist's POV?"
"Make this scene second-person for a more immersive experience."

☑ Checklist: Keeping POV Consistent

- ☑ Stay inside the **chosen character's awareness**
- ☑ Avoid describing other characters' **private thoughts** unless omniscient
- ☑ Use **language, tone, and sensory details** that reflect the POV character
- ☑ Ask: *Would this character realistically know or perceive this right now?*

Refinement Prompts

- "Highlight any POV slips in this chapter."
- "Rewrite this to stay emotionally close to the narrator."
- "Improve the flow of internal thoughts without over-explaining."
- "Add more sensory detail from the character's perspective."

"Point of view isn't just where your story is told from—it's where your reader lives."

Foreshadowing, Pacing & Subplots

Crafting a Multi-Layered Story with Momentum and Meaning

These three elements—**foreshadowing**, **pacing**, and **subplots**—are often what separate a good book from a great one. They add emotional tension, complexity, and a satisfying sense of cohesion to your storytelling. When used with intention, they make your narrative feel deliberate, immersive, and rewarding to reread.

ChatGPT can help you design and refine these layers so they integrate naturally with your main plot, resonate with your themes, and keep your reader hooked.

Foreshadowing: Planting Seeds Early

Foreshadowing involves **hints or clues** about what's to come. When done well, it creates suspense, builds emotional investment, and delivers satisfying payoffs.

Prompt Examples:

- "Suggest 3 ways I can subtly foreshadow a betrayal in Chapter 8 during Chapters 1–3."
- "I want a major twist to feel earned. How can I plant early clues that won't give it away?"
- "List small character behaviors or setting details that could hint at a future reveal."

Pacing: Managing Momentum

Pacing determines **how fast or slow your story unfolds**, and when to speed up or slow down for emotional impact. ChatGPT can help you analyze or adjust your pacing to avoid flat sections or rushed climaxes.

Prompt Examples:

- "Review this chapter and suggest where I should slow down or speed up the pacing."
- "Add a quiet emotional beat between these two action scenes to allow readers to breathe."
- "Make this moment feel more urgent by tightening the language and shortening the sentences."

Subplots: Deepening Theme and Character

Subplots are secondary storylines that support or contrast with the main plot. They help:

- Develop side characters
- Reinforce your core themes
- Add complexity and realism
- Delay or deepen the main conflict

Prompt Examples:

- "Create a subplot for my main character's best friend that mirrors the theme of forgiveness."
- "Give me 2 ideas for a romantic subplot that doesn't overshadow the main quest."
- "How can I tie this subplot back into the main story arc for a stronger emotional climax?"

Checklist: Strong Narrative Layering

Element	Goal	AI Prompt Example
Foreshadowing	Build anticipation	"Hide a clue about the ending in a symbolic object."
Pacing	Balance tension and release	"Slow the scene down by focusing on sensory detail."
Subplots	Enhance complexity	"Give the antagonist a subplot that humanizes them."

Refinement Prompts

- "Where can I add foreshadowing in this first act?"
- "Make this scene feel more suspenseful through pacing."
- "Suggest ways to merge this subplot with the climax."
- "Trim this subplot so it doesn't derail the main narrative."

"Foreshadowing gives your story gravity. Pacing gives it breath. Subplots give it soul."

Prompt Examples:

"Describe a fantasy town with X features..."

Crafting Vivid Settings with Targeted Prompts

Setting is more than just background—it's a living part of your story. With the right prompt, ChatGPT can help you describe **entire towns, cities, or regions** that feel immersive, symbolic, and aligned with your genre.

This is especially valuable in **fantasy, sci-fi, historical fiction, or magical realism**, where the setting helps define the mood, culture, and even the plot mechanics.

Prompt Structure: Customizing Your World

Start by identifying key features you want included:

- **Genre** (fantasy, steampunk, dystopian, etc.)
- **Mood or tone** (mysterious, sacred, eerie, joyful)
- **Geography** (mountains, coastal, desert, forest)
- **Function** (trading town, mystical village, political hub)
- **Unique feature** (floating buildings, glowing plants, living statues)

Sample Prompts You Can Use

1. **"Describe a fantasy mountain town built into the cliffside, known for its crystal mining and ancient healing springs."**
2. **"Create a medieval village where people whisper about a cursed forest nearby. Include details about the buildings, market, and daily life."**
3. **"Design a steampunk city powered by wind turbines and gears, with foggy canals and rooftop gardens."**

4. **"Describe a hidden town in the desert that only appears during full moons. Include visuals, culture, and town legends."**
5. **"Give me a cozy, autumn-themed village for a fantasy romance. Include color palettes, scents, seasonal foods, and local events."**

Refinement Prompts for Depth

- "Add tension or mystery to this town's atmosphere."
- "Include cultural traditions or taboos specific to this region."
- "Make the town feel magical but grounded in realism."
- "Give the village a dark secret that locals don't speak about."
- "Turn this into a travel guide excerpt for a character's journal."

☑ Checklist: A Strong Setting Description Includes…

- ☑ **Sensory detail** (smells, colors, sounds)
- ☑ **Geography and architecture**
- ☑ **Cultural flavor** (traditions, clothing, food)
- ☑ **Conflict or contrast** (something unusual, hidden, or off)
- ☑ **Relevance to story or character**

Bonus Application: Worldbuilding Journals or Extras

These descriptive outputs can also be used for:

- Companion world guides
- Interactive maps or illustrations
- Bonus content for superfans
- Immersion in role-playing or gamified books

"A well-drawn town doesn't just house the story—it holds its soul."

CHAPTER 7: Special Sections for Nonfiction

Establishing Credibility

Position Yourself as a Trusted Voice in Your Genre

Whether you're writing nonfiction, memoir, or even fiction that draws on real-world experience, **credibility builds trust** with your reader. When readers believe in your authority, they're more likely to follow your insights, recommend your work, and view you as a thought leader.

ChatGPT can assist you in **clarifying your voice, credentials, and experience**—and expressing them strategically in your writing, bio, and marketing content.

Why Credibility Matters

- For **nonfiction**, it validates your knowledge and strengthens your argument
- For **memoir**, it builds emotional trust in your lived experience
- Even in **fiction**, showing research and world expertise adds realism
- In **marketing**, it increases media interest, partnerships, and book sales

Prompt Examples to Establish Credibility

In Your Book's Voice or Content:

- "Help me write an introductory paragraph that shows my experience without sounding boastful."
- "Rewrite this section to reflect that I have 20+ years in holistic health education."
- "Suggest a way to include my client case studies or research in this chapter."
- "Turn my resume highlights into a bio suitable for a nonfiction book on [topic]."

For Author Pages and Promotional Material:

- "Write a professional bio for my website based on these credentials: [paste details]."
- "Create an elevator pitch that positions me as an expert in [industry/topic]."
- "Suggest testimonials or endorsement ideas that reinforce my expertise."

Ways to Show Credibility in Your Writing

Strategy	Example
Tell a story that illustrates your experience	"I remember when I first started my healing practice in 1998..."
Reference credentials naturally	"As a Doctor of Natural Medicine, I've witnessed this transformation firsthand."
Share relevant research or case studies	"In a 2023 meta-study on energy medicine, researchers found…"

Strategy	Example
Use confident, clear language	Avoid hedging terms like "maybe" or "I think" unless stylistically intended
Offer valuable insight up front	Teach before you pitch—offer proof of value in your writing itself

ChatGPT Tip:

Ask ChatGPT to identify credibility gaps in your writing or to suggest where you could **add authority without overexplaining**. Prompt:
"Review this chapter and suggest one way I could strengthen my credibility without listing more credentials."

☑ Checklist: Credibility Builders

- ☑ Qualifications or credentials relevant to the topic
- ☑ Real-life experience, stories, or client work
- ☑ Testimonials or endorsements (optional but powerful)
- ☑ Confident tone—avoiding apology or vagueness
- ☑ Clear understanding of the reader's needs

"Credibility isn't about proving yourself—it's about showing up with earned wisdom, ready to serve."

Teaching Through Storytelling
Transforming Information into Impact

Stories aren't just for fiction—they're one of the most **powerful tools for teaching**, especially in nonfiction, personal development, wellness, or business writing. If you want your ideas to resonate and stick, **wrap them in a narrative**.

Teaching through storytelling helps your readers:

- Understand complex concepts
- Connect emotionally to the content
- Remember key lessons long after reading

And ChatGPT can help you find, craft, and refine the stories that bring your teaching to life.

Why Storytelling Works

Humans are wired for story. The brain processes narrative differently than raw facts:

- It creates **emotional engagement**
- Helps make **meaning from abstract ideas**
- Provides **real-life context** and relatability
- Turns advice into **transformational insight**

Prompt Examples for Teaching Through Story

- "Help me create a short story that demonstrates the concept of energetic boundaries in healing."
- "Give me a parable or metaphor for explaining how intuition works."
- "Turn this list of wellness tips into a narrative where a client goes through a transformation."
- "Write a fictional story that teaches the principles of writing discipline without sounding preachy."

- "Can you turn my bullet-point list into a real-life scenario with dialogue and emotional learning?"

Story Formats You Can Use

Format	Example Use
Personal Anecdote	"When I launched my first book, I had no idea how to market it…"
Client Transformation	"Sophia walked into my clinic overwhelmed. Three weeks later…"
Fictional Example	"Meet Maya—a healer who had no idea she was absorbing her clients' energy."
Parable or Fable	"Once there was a candle that refused to burn, afraid of using its wax…"
Case Study	"Let's look at what happened when one coach used AI to map out her course launch."

ChatGPT Prompt for Discovery

"I want to teach [your lesson]. Ask me questions to draw out a personal story, fictional example, or metaphor I can use to illustrate it."

Then follow up with:

"Now write that as a 500-word story in my voice and make the takeaway clear but natural."

☑ Checklist: Strong Teaching Stories Should…

- ☑ Have a **relatable character** or scenario
- ☑ Show a **challenge or question** the reader might face
- ☑ Deliver the **lesson organically** through action or dialogue
- ☑ Feel aligned with the **tone and theme** of your book
- ☑ End with **emotional resolution or insight**

Refinement Prompts

- "Make this story more emotional without sounding exaggerated."
- "Can you add dialogue to make it more immersive?"
- "Turn this into a teaching moment without losing the narrative flow."
- "Suggest a metaphorical version of this for spiritual readers."

"The mind may understand information, but the heart remembers stories."

Creating Diagrams or Frameworks with AI

Visualizing Ideas for Clarity, Teaching & Engagement

As an author—especially in nonfiction, self-help, or educational genres—**visual frameworks** can turn abstract ideas into clear, structured, memorable content. Diagrams, models, and flowcharts simplify learning, deepen understanding, and give your reader an easy way to recall your message.

While ChatGPT can't create finished graphic visuals directly, it **can help you build the structure**, layout, and language needed for your **designer** or for tools like Canva, Lucidchart, or PowerPoint.

WHY USE FRAMEWORKS IN YOUR BOOK?

- Breaks complex ideas into digestible parts
- Adds visual variation to your layout
- Makes your teachings feel original, organized, and "ownable"
- Appeals to **visual learners** and supports retention

Prompt Examples for Creating Frameworks

"Can you create a 4-part framework to explain how authors can use AI in writing?"
"Suggest a diagram layout for teaching the five layers of energy healing."
"Turn these bullet points into a triangle model with three pillars."
"Build me a chart comparing traditional publishing vs. self-publishing."
"Give me a visual map showing the stages of writing a book with AI support."

Popular Framework Types You Can Generate with AI

Framework Type	Example Use	Prompt
Pyramid or Hierarchy	Maslow-style needs, levels of mastery	"Organize the writing journey into 5 ascending levels."
Circle/Wheel	Holistic or cyclical concepts	"Create a wellness model showing how sleep, nutrition, and mindset support writing flow."
Venn Diagram	Showing overlap or integration	"Show where intuition, creativity, and AI intersect in storytelling."
Grid/Matrix	Compare variables or traits	"Map out 4 writing styles based on speed and emotional depth."
Flowchart	Step-by-step processes	"Outline the AI-assisted publishing process in 7 steps."

Refinement Prompts

- "Can you label each section with a keyword and short phrase?"
- "Write a brief paragraph explaining each part of the framework."
- "Suggest names for this model that make it sound original and branded."
- "Make it suitable for use in a workshop slide or book diagram."

- "Turn this into a boxed insert or pull-out graphic for the book."

☑ Checklist: Effective Diagrams Should...

- ☑ Be simple, intuitive, and skimmable
- ☑ Represent a core idea, process, or relationship
- ☑ Use clear and distinct parts or phases
- ☑ Tie directly into your book's message or theme
- ☑ Be explainable in both **visual** and **verbal** form

Bonus Tip: Visual Style Consistency

When you're ready to design, bring your AI-generated framework to life using:

- **Canva** (templates, shapes, icons)
- **Lucidchart / Whimsical** (interactive flowcharts or diagrams)
- **PowerPoint / Keynote** (clean, professional layouts)
- **Fiverr or Upwork** (hire a diagram illustrator using your AI outline)

"When your ideas are seen and not just read, they live longer in the minds of your readers."

Organizing Case Studies, Stats, and Stories

Bringing Evidence, Emotion, and Engagement Together

Whether you're writing nonfiction, a how-to guide, a wellness book, or a business strategy manual, the **most impactful writing blends logic and emotion**—and that often comes through in the way you present **case studies, statistics, and stories**.

This trio gives your book:

- **Credibility** (through data)
- **Relatability** (through stories)
- **Clarity** (through real-world examples)

ChatGPT can help you **structure**, **enhance**, and even **generate templates** for these elements, so your chapters feel trustworthy and engaging—not like a data dump or a disconnected narrative.

Why Balance All Three?

Element	Purpose	Example
Stat/Data	Proves the point objectively	"78% of authors feel blocked while drafting."
Case Study	Shows it applied in real life	"Emma used a 3-prompt sequence to write her memoir in 6 months."
Story	Creates emotional connection	"At first, she didn't even call herself a writer…"

Together, they build a **trust bridge** between you and your reader.

ChatGPT Prompt Examples

For Outlining a Case Study:

"Help me write a 500-word case study of an author who used AI to overcome writer's block and complete their book. Make it believable, emotionally engaging, and useful."

For Generating Relevant Stats:

"Give me 5 current statistics about self-publishing success rates with sources I can verify."
"Summarize key industry data about AI use in creative fields."

For Storytelling Support:

"Write a short narrative about a first-time children's author discovering ChatGPT."
"Turn this client transformation [paste details] into a mini story with a before/after arc."

How to Structure a Case Study (with AI Support)

1. **Introduction** – Who is this person/group? Why are they relevant?
2. **Challenge** – What problem or goal were they facing?
3. **Solution** – What did they do (especially involving AI, your method, or your system)?
4. **Result** – What changed? Include emotional and measurable outcomes.
5. **Lesson or Takeaway** – What can the reader apply from this?

Prompt:

"Can you turn this information into a case study using the 5-part format?"

Organizing These Elements in Your Book

Placement Strategy	How to Use It
Chapter Openers	Start with a story or statistic to hook readers
Inserts or Sidebars	Break up text with case examples
End-of-Chapter Lessons	Tie together the stat, case, and story with a takeaway
Pull Quotes	Use the most impactful line or data point visually
Infographics	Turn stats into engaging visuals (ChatGPT + Canva combo)

Refinement Prompts

- "Make this case study more emotional while staying professional."
- "Add a quote from the person in the story to make it feel real."
- "Turn this stat into a compelling sentence I can put in my introduction."
- "Suggest how to connect this case to my reader's journey."

"Facts tell. Stories sell. Together, they teach."

Prompt Examples:

"List Key Points for a Chapter on..."

Outlining Chapters with Clarity, Speed, and Precision

Once you've got your chapter title or main idea, the next step is **figuring out what to include**. This is where ChatGPT shines as your brainstorming assistant — helping you break down a broad topic into **teachable points**, **sections**, or **scene beats**, depending on your genre.

Asking ChatGPT to "list key points for a chapter on..." gives you an instant roadmap. Whether you're outlining nonfiction, developing scenes for fiction, or building a children's book with bite-sized lessons, this one simple prompt opens the door to a **structured writing plan**.

Sample Prompts You Can Use

FOR NONFICTION:

"List the key points I should include in a chapter on the power of visualization for goal-setting."
"What are the essential elements in a chapter about creating a self-care routine for busy entrepreneurs?"
"Give me a breakdown for a chapter titled 'Healing Through the Five Elements' for holistic health readers."

FOR FICTION:

"List the main emotional and plot beats in a chapter where my heroine discovers a secret about her past."
"What key points should I cover in a scene that introduces the villain without giving too much away?"

FOR CHILDREN'S BOOKS:

"List the key ideas to include in a story teaching kids about bravery at bedtime, for ages 4–6."
"What are the developmental goals I should cover in a chapter on friendship for early readers?"

ChatGPT Can Help You:

- Generate **subheadings or section titles**
- Offer **sequencing advice** (what to explain first, second, third)
- Suggest **supporting material** like case studies, data, or metaphors
- Warn about **redundancy or overlap** with other chapters
- Fill in **gaps** you might not think to include

Example:

Prompt:

"List key points for a chapter on 'Grounding Techniques for Empaths.'"

Response Might Include:

1. What grounding is and why it's important for empaths
2. Physical grounding vs. energetic grounding
3. Techniques (e.g., breathwork, crystals, visualization)
4. When to ground (daily, after sessions, in crowds)
5. Misconceptions and what to avoid
6. How to teach grounding to clients or children
7. Reflection prompts or journaling exercises
8. Resources for continued support

You can then ask:

"Now turn each of those points into a paragraph summary."
"Add an example story for point 3."
"Create subheadings from those eight points."

Refinement Prompts

- "Expand this list into a full chapter outline."
- "Which of these should come first and why?"
- "Make this list more advanced—assume the reader is already familiar with the basics."
- "Now write this like it's for beginners."
- "Which point could become a chapter on its own?"

"One great prompt can unlock the entire structure of your next chapter."

CHAPTER 8: Special Sections for Children's Books

Language and Sentence Complexity by Age Group

Crafting Age-Appropriate Language with AI Support

One of the most important aspects of writing children's books is **understanding how language evolves with age**. What's engaging for a 3-year-old may bore or confuse a 7-year-old. The tone, vocabulary, sentence structure, and even **moral complexity** must be tailored to match a child's **cognitive, emotional, and literacy development**.

ChatGPT can help you adjust your writing to **meet age-specific needs**, suggest alternatives, and ensure your story remains developmentally appropriate and easy to follow.

Age Group Breakdown: Language & Sentence Expectations

Age Group	Key Language Features	Sentence Complexity
0–3 years (*Board Books*)	Repetition, rhyme, sound words (onomatopoeia), naming objects	One to two words per page or very short phrases. Often one concept per page.
3–5 years (*Picture Books*)	Simple vocabulary, familiar topics, playful tone, emotional themes (like sharing, friendship)	One short sentence per page or simple two-part sentences. Rhythm and rhyme common.
5–7 years (*Early Readers*)	Sight words, basic storytelling, simple cause-effect logic	Short sentences with basic punctuation. Some dialogue. May include 100–500 words total.
7–9 years (*Chapter Books*)	Imaginative narratives, some moral themes, character development begins	Paragraph-length sentences, limited figurative language, around 1,000–10,000 words total
9–12 years (*Middle Grade*)	Deeper themes (identity, justice), stronger character arcs, humor, conflict	Full-length paragraphs, varied sentence structure, subplots emerge. 10,000–50,000+ words.
13+ (*Young Adult*)	Sarcasm, identity crisis, complex emotion, romance, societal themes	Adult-level sentence structure, internal monologue, flashbacks, layered subtext. 50k–100k+ words.

Prompt Examples You Can Use

"Rewrite this paragraph so it's suitable for a 4-year-old."
"Simplify this dialogue for a 6-year-old and make it more playful."
"What words or themes should I avoid for children aged 5–7?"
"Adjust this story to match the vocabulary level of a 3rd grader."
"List common sentence structures used in early reader books."
"Can you show me how this sentence would look for ages 3–5, 7–9, and 10–12?"

Tips for Prompting by Age Level

- Specify the **exact age or grade** level you're targeting
- Mention whether you want **rhyme, repetition, or dialogue**
- If applicable, include **word count limits** or reading level (e.g., Lexile, Flesch-Kincaid)

Example: "Turn this story into a 200-word bedtime picture book for ages 3–5, using repetition and rhyming words."

Checklist: Age-Appropriate Writing Includes…

- Vocabulary that matches cognitive development
- Themes children can relate to in their daily lives
- Short, clear sentence structures
- Emotional tone that supports learning or safety
- Avoidance of abstract metaphors (for very young children)
- Rhythm or rhyme (especially for pre-K and early reader groups)

"Writing for children is not about dumbing down — it's about tuning in."

Rhyme Schemes & Rhythm

Creating Musical Language That Captivates Young Readers

Rhyme and rhythm are the heartbeat of many children's books — especially for ages 0–7. These elements not only **make stories fun to read aloud**, but also help young readers **develop phonemic awareness**, memory, and a love for language.

When using ChatGPT to assist with rhyming stories, it helps to understand basic rhyme patterns and rhythmic structure so you can prompt with clarity and precision.

WHY RHYME AND RHYTHM MATTER IN KIDS' BOOKS

- Enhances memory and word retention
- Makes read-alouds musical and engaging
- Supports early language development
- Reinforces natural language flow and speech patterns
- Helps parents and children bond during reading time

Common Rhyme Schemes

Scheme	Pattern
AABB	Lines rhyme in pairs
The dog ran fast / He had a blast	
He chased a cat / Then lost his hat	
ABAB	Alternating rhymes
The moon was high / The night was still	

Scheme	Pattern
Stars lit the sky / Above the hill	
ABCB	Only 2nd and 4th lines rhyme
He found a trail / So wild and wide	
He walked it slow / And laughed with pride	
AABBA (Limerick)	Classic 5-line humorous rhyme
There once was a frog on a log	
Who danced with a cat and a dog	
They spun in the rain / With joy and no pain	
Then slipped in the mud with a "splat" and a fog!	

What Is Rhythm?

Rhythm refers to the **beat and meter** of your sentences. Like music, it follows a pattern. In writing, we often use **syllables** and **stress patterns**.

Common Rhythmic Patterns:

- **Iambic** (da-DUM): *"I think I saw a little cat"*
- **Trochaic** (DA-dum): *"Happy people run and play"*
- **Anapestic** (da-da-DUM): *"In the light of the moon"*

- **Dactylic** (DA-da-da): *"Happily skipping through fields"*

Even if you don't know these terms, ChatGPT can match your preferred rhythm if you describe it clearly.

Prompt Examples to Try

"Write a 4-line AABB rhyme about a curious mouse exploring the world."
"Create a rhyming paragraph in an ABAB scheme for a bedtime story."
"Help me write a 6-line rhyme with a gentle rhythm for toddlers."
"Can you improve the meter in this poem to make it flow more naturally?"
"Fix this verse so it follows a consistent iambic pattern."
"Suggest alternative rhymes for 'tree' and 'light.'"

Editing Prompts for Rhythm & Flow

- "Make this rhyme more natural and less forced."
- "Adjust the rhythm to be smoother for reading aloud."
- "Suggest better end rhymes that don't sound predictable."
- "Add internal rhymes or playful repetition."
- "Simplify the vocabulary for 4–5 year olds."

Rhyme & Rhythm Best Practices:

- Avoid overly complex or awkward rhymes
- Read aloud for flow and pacing
- Don't sacrifice **story** for rhyme — keep meaning intact
- Use repetition sparingly for rhythm reinforcement
- Let the rhyme support — not dominate — your message

"When rhyme and rhythm come together, they sing the story into a child's heart."

Picture Book Structure

Building Page-Turning Magic for Young Minds

Writing a picture book is both an art and a blueprint. You're not just telling a story — you're crafting a visual and emotional journey, typically in **32 pages or fewer**, where every word counts and every page turn matters. Structure provides the framework that lets your creativity soar — and ChatGPT can help you build that structure with precision and playfulness.

Standard Picture Book Format: The 32-Page Blueprint

Most traditionally published picture books follow a **32-page format**. Here's how it usually breaks down:

Page(s)	Purpose
1	Title page
2–3	Dedication / Copyright / Optional opening
4–5	**Beginning**: Introduce main character & setting
6–13	Introduce conflict, establish the problem
14–23	**Middle**: Escalation, setbacks, character growth
24–29	**Climax**: Turning point, resolution begins
30–31	**Ending**: Full resolution, emotional payoff
32	Closing image or final twist (or blank for publishing needs)

Remember: Not every story fits this model exactly, but it's a helpful guide — especially if you're working with illustrators or aiming to submit to publishers.

Key Story Elements in Picture Books

- **Character**: Clear, relatable, and usually childlike in emotion (even if they're animals or objects).
- **Conflict**: A single central problem (e.g., lost teddy, fear of the dark, first day of school).
- **Resolution**: Simple, satisfying solution the child could understand or learn from.
- **Emotion**: Picture books must touch the heart — even silly ones!
- **Repetition or Pattern**: Children love structure — try repeated lines, counting, or question-answer patterns.
- **Visual Cues**: Leave room for the **illustrator** to tell half the story.

ChatGPT Prompts for Picture Book Planning

"Help me outline a 32-page picture book about a girl who plants kindness seeds."
"Suggest a beginning, middle, and end for a story teaching bravery using a bunny as the main character."
"What should happen on each page of a story about a turtle learning to ask for help?"
"Turn this summary into a 12-spread picture book structure with page turns in mind."
"Suggest where page turns would add suspense or humor in this story: [paste draft]."

Advanced Tips: How to Prompt Like a Picture Book Pro

- Ask ChatGPT to separate **"what's written"** vs. **"what's illustrated."**
- Prompt for **emotional beats** — especially on pages 14, 24, and 31.
- Request **rhyming vs. prose** versions to compare tone.

- If working with an illustrator, ask:

  "Suggest visual cues for each page of this story."

☑ Picture Book Planning Checklist:

- ☑ One clear theme or emotional takeaway
- ☑ Character growth that's easy for children to grasp
- ☑ Simple sentence structure and age-appropriate vocabulary
- ☑ Strategic page turns for rhythm, surprise, or humor
- ☑ Minimal text per page — 50–250 words total for most

"A picture book is a dance between words and images — and every beat must matter."

ChatGPT + Image Prompts (for Illustrated Books)

Bringing Your Story to Life with Visual AI Collaboration

Illustrated books — from children's stories to graphic guides — rely as much on **images** as they do on text. Whether you're working with an illustrator or generating your own AI art, ChatGPT can **help you craft precise image prompts** that guide your visual storytelling. When paired with image-generation tools (like DALL·E, Midjourney, or Canva AI), your ideas can take shape faster and clearer than ever before.

WHY USE CHATGPT FOR IMAGE PROMPTING?

ChatGPT helps you:

- Clarify visual ideas (e.g., "a shy elephant under a polka-dot umbrella")
- Create detailed scene descriptions to hand to illustrators or AI tools
- Stay consistent with color schemes, character design, and mood
- Ensure illustrations are **age-appropriate**, emotionally resonant, and aligned with the book's tone

What Makes a Good Image Prompt?

Whether you're using an illustrator or AI generator, the best prompts include:

- **Subject**: Who or what is in the scene?
- **Action**: What are they doing?
- **Setting**: Where is it happening?
- **Mood/Style**: Is it cozy, whimsical, mysterious?

- **Art Style**: Cartoon, watercolor, flat vector, pencil sketch?
- **Color Palette**: Soft pastels, bold primaries, muted earth tones?

Prompt Examples for ChatGPT to Refine

"Help me describe an illustration for page 5 of my picture book: the main character, a bunny named Max, is looking for his lost carrot in a windy meadow."
"Turn this scene into an image prompt I can give to an AI art generator."
"Give me a visual prompt for a 5-year-old's picture book about a dinosaur learning to swim."
"Describe a warm, cozy forest at sunset with gentle magical elements, suitable for a bedtime book illustration."
"What are some age-appropriate illustration ideas for a story about gratitude for ages 4–6?"

Example: From Story Scene to Visual Prompt

Scene:
A little girl and her dog are reading under a blanket fort lit by fairy lights.

ChatGPT Visual Prompt:

"A young girl with curly brown hair and pajamas reads a picture book inside a homemade blanket fort. Her golden retriever lies beside her, head on her lap. The fort is glowing with string lights, and books and plush toys are scattered around. Style: watercolor illustration, warm tones, cozy evening mood."

For Authors Working With Human Illustrators

ChatGPT can also help generate:

- **Illustration briefs** (scene-by-scene)

- **Character sheets** (poses, outfits, color references)
- **Mood boards descriptions**
- **Consistency checks** across the book

Prompt:

"Create a list of all the illustrated scenes I should include in a 12-page children's book about a cat that wants to fly."

BONUS TIP: Pairing with Image AI

Once ChatGPT gives you a refined prompt, copy it into your preferred visual AI tool (like DALL·E 3 in ChatGPT Plus, Midjourney, or Canva AI). You can even ask ChatGPT to generate **multiple variations** for testing different tones or styles.

Combine with Text for a Complete Creative Vision

Pair each visual prompt with the text that appears on that page. This ensures:

- Cohesive storytelling
- Balanced image-to-word ratio
- A smooth flow from spread to spread

"Illustration isn't just decoration — it's storytelling without words. Let AI help you visualize what your heart imagines."

Moral Lessons & Message Clarity

Crafting Purposeful Stories That Resonate and Teach

Children's books often do more than entertain — they **teach**, **nurture**, and **shape values**. Whether you're writing a tale about honesty, kindness, bravery, or patience, the moral or message of your story should be **clear, age-appropriate, and emotionally grounded**.

With ChatGPT, you can refine your book's core message, ensure it's woven naturally into the story, and avoid sounding preachy or overly obvious. The goal is to **inspire understanding**, not deliver a lecture.

Why Moral Lessons Matter in Children's Books

- **Foundation for Character Development**
  Children absorb messages through story-based learning far better than through direct instruction.
- **Reinforces Social & Emotional Learning (SEL)**
  Themes like empathy, inclusion, courage, or resilience help kids navigate real-life challenges.
- **Shapes Worldview**
  Stories influence how young readers view others, themselves, and the world around them.

Characteristics of Effective Moral Messaging

- Woven seamlessly into the story
- Demonstrated through **character actions and consequences**
- Age-appropriate complexity (simpler for younger children, layered for older readers)

- Universal themes that don't rely on cultural or religious assumptions (unless intended)
- Gentle tone — no preaching or "telling"

ChatGPT Prompt Examples

"What moral lesson could I teach in a story about a dragon who's afraid to fly?"

"Suggest three endings that reinforce the message of sharing in a 5-year-old's picture book."

"Rewrite this story to more clearly show the theme of friendship without saying it outright."

"How can I show forgiveness through the actions of two raccoon characters fighting over food?"

"Can you help me brainstorm moral takeaways for a story about moving to a new home?"

"Make the message of this story more subtle but still emotionally clear."

Ideas for Popular Themes by Age Group

Age Group	Common Moral Themes
2–4	Sharing, patience, helping others, being gentle
5–7	Friendship, honesty, perseverance, bravery
8–10	Fairness, inclusion, dealing with change, consequences
10–12	Self-worth, independence, empathy, ethical choices

Tools ChatGPT Can Provide

- **Moral message analysis**: Ask "What is the takeaway from this story?"
- **Dialogue that reveals character change**
- **Story arc suggestions** to emphasize growth without overt moralizing
- **Alternatives to clichéd messaging** that still hit the emotional mark

Checklist for Message Clarity

- Is the message demonstrated through action rather than explained?
- Can a child retell the lesson in their own words?
- Are the emotional stakes high enough to make the message meaningful?
- Is the message age-appropriate without being too simplistic?

"The best stories teach without teaching — they guide hearts by walking beside them."

CHAPTER 9: Finalizing the Manuscript

Using ChatGPT to Create a Style Guide for Your Book

Establishing Voice, Formatting, and Creative Consistency from Start to Finish

Whether you're writing fiction, nonfiction, or a children's book, a **style guide** is your behind-the-scenes blueprint. It ensures your book remains **consistent in voice, tone, terminology, formatting, character traits, spelling choices, and more** — especially if your project spans months, involves editors or collaborators, or includes sequels or companion materials.

ChatGPT can help you **build your own customized style guide**, maintain it, and refer back to it throughout your writing and editing process.

WHAT IS A BOOK STYLE GUIDE?

A **style guide** is a working document that outlines your creative and editorial decisions, such as:

- Character voice, habits, backstories, quirks
- Preferred spelling or grammar rules (e.g., US vs. Canadian English)
- Consistent terminology (especially in nonfiction)
- Tone and language level (e.g., formal vs. conversational)

- Formatting rules (italics, footnotes, capitalization, etc.)
- Punctuation preferences (e.g., Oxford comma, dash vs. ellipsis)

ChatGPT Prompt Examples

"Help me create a style guide for my nonfiction book on holistic healing."
"List the tone, voice, and vocabulary I've used so far in this story: [paste excerpt]."
"Create a character consistency chart for my main characters based on these descriptions."
"List all the key terms in my manuscript and define them in a glossary format."
"Suggest a formatting style for headings, subheadings, and callout boxes."
"Can you help me write style rules for dialogue punctuation in my middle-grade novel?"
"Analyze this writing sample and summarize the style, tone, and rhythm I'm using."

Use Cases for a Style Guide

Use Case	Benefit
Long projects	Prevent drift in tone or structure
Working with editors or ghostwriters	Keeps external help aligned
Nonfiction & instructional books	Ensures accuracy and terminology clarity
Series or sequels	Keeps continuity across volumes
Translations & formatting	Saves time and confusion during layout or internationalization

Sections You Can Include in Your Guide

1. **Voice & Tone Overview**
2. **Audience Persona (Reading Level, Expectations)**
3. **Vocabulary / Glossary of Terms**
4. **Formatting Rules (for headings, quotes, captions, etc.)**
5. **Grammar & Spelling Preferences**
6. **Punctuation Guidelines**
7. **Character Profiles (for fiction)**
8. **Common Phrases or Repetitions to Avoid**
9. **Dialogue Style Rules**
10. **Citation Style (APA, MLA, Chicago, etc., if applicable)**

How to Use ChatGPT Throughout

- Start by saying:

  "I'm writing a [type of book], and I want to stay consistent. Help me create a style guide."

- Then ask section by section, or provide excerpts and say:

  "Summarize the voice and tone I'm using."
  "What grammar or spelling rules are consistent in this draft?"
  "Suggest a format for chapter titles and subtitles."
  "Create a glossary for these terms: [list terms]."

Update your style guide as your book evolves. You can even ask ChatGPT to keep track of changes or recheck for inconsistencies using past content.

"A style guide is the invisible thread that ties your book together — with AI, it becomes easier than ever to stay on track creatively."

Proofreading with AI: What It Can & Can't Do

Using ChatGPT to Polish Your Prose — While Knowing Its Limits

AI tools like ChatGPT can be incredibly helpful when it comes to **light proofreading, grammar refinement, and tone smoothing**. But it's important to know where AI shines — and where you still need a human eye.

Think of AI proofreading as your **first line of editing**: fast, accessible, and capable of catching many common errors. But when it comes to nuance, context, or industry-specific style guides, a professional editor or proofreader may still be essential — especially for published books.

WHAT CHATGPT CAN DO FOR PROOFREADING

- **Fix grammar and punctuation errors**
- **Reword clunky or awkward phrasing**
- **Improve sentence flow and clarity**
- **Correct inconsistent verb tense and perspective**
- **Make passive voice more active**
- **Catch basic typos, repeated words, or misplaced modifiers**
- **Adjust tone for different audiences** (e.g., more professional, more casual)
- **Flag overuse of adverbs or filler words**
- **Summarize or simplify overly complex sentences**

Prompt examples:
"Proofread this paragraph for grammar, punctuation, and clarity."
"Make this sound smoother and more natural."
"Remove redundancies and tighten the writing in this section."
"Does anything in this passage sound off or confusing?"
"Highlight passive voice and suggest active alternatives."

What ChatGPT Can't Reliably Do (Yet)

- **Catch subtle errors in context or meaning** (e.g., "there" vs. "their" used correctly but confusingly)
- **Understand tone shifts across an entire manuscript**
- **Follow your personal or publisher's style guide** without explicit direction
- **Verify factual accuracy or data integrity**
- **Proof visual formatting (e.g., headings, spacing, layout)**
- **Replace the creative judgment of a human editor**
- **Handle niche language or jargon with precision**
- **Pick up on authorial voice changes across chapters**

When to Combine AI + Human Editing

Use AI For...	Use a Human For...
First-pass proofreading	Final proof before publication
Tightening messy paragraphs	Nuance, humor, and creative rhythm
Consistency in terms or phrasing	Style, structure, and thematic flow
Speed and affordability	Deep edits for market-readiness

Tip: Give ChatGPT Specific Instructions

The more context you provide, the better your results. For example:

"Proofread this paragraph for a children's picture book, keeping the language playful and age-appropriate."
"Fix grammar and tighten the tone, but don't change my voice — this is for a romantic fiction novel."
"Edit this in Canadian English and follow APA citation formatting."

AI Proofreading Workflow Suggestion

1. **Paste a section** (250–500 words at a time works best)
2. Ask ChatGPT to:
   - Proofread for errors
   - Suggest tone improvements
   - Highlight wordy or confusing sections
3. Apply changes as needed
4. Repeat as you build your draft
5. Do a full human read-through at the end

Other Helpful Editing Tools for Authors

Tool	Strengths	Weaknesses
Grammarly	Real-time grammar checks, clarity suggestions, tone analysis	Can be overly aggressive; may "flatten" creative voice
ProWritingAid	Deep style reports, readability stats, in-depth editing across long texts	Slight learning curve; can feel technical
Hemingway Editor	Highlights readability, sentence complexity, passive voice	Best for simplifying; less helpful with nuanced tone
QuillBot	Rewriting, paraphrasing, vocabulary improvement	Can sound robotic if overused
WordRake (for Word users)	Legal and business writing polish	Not ideal for fiction or narrative content

Workflow Tip: Combine Tools Strategically

You don't need to choose just one — here's a simple **editing stack** many authors use:

1. **Draft in Word / Google Docs** or with ChatGPT
2. Run sections through **Grammarly** or **ProWritingAid**
3. Use **Hemingway** to simplify dense areas
4. Ask **ChatGPT** for tone/style/flow edits
5. Final read-through by **a human proofreader** (or yourself after a break)

Final Tips

- Save your **style preferences** in Grammarly or ChatGPT prompts (e.g., "Canadian English, casual tone, nonfiction guidebook")
- Use **track changes** when possible to preserve your voice and stay in control of edits
- Always **read aloud** your final draft — AI can't hear rhythm or pacing like you can

"AI can catch what your eyes gloss over — but your heart, your rhythm, and your message still need *you.*"

Beta Reader Feedback with ChatGPT (Simulated Feedback)

How to Simulate Honest Reader Reactions Before You Hit "Publish"

Beta readers are invaluable — they help you see your manuscript through a reader's eyes, catching **plot holes, emotional gaps, pacing issues, or confusion** long before critics do. But what if you don't have a full team of trusted readers (yet)? That's where **ChatGPT can simulate beta reader feedback** in a fast, structured, and customizable way.

While it's not a substitute for real human feedback, it *can* offer powerful insight — especially when you know how to prompt it correctly.

What Simulated Beta Feedback Can Help With

- Spotting **plot holes or inconsistencies**
- Highlighting **unclear character motivations**
- Noticing **confusing transitions or pacing dips**
- Catching **underdeveloped subplots or themes**
- Giving emotional reactions: "As a reader, this made me feel…"
- Suggesting which parts are **slow, powerful, or confusing**
- Offering feedback **by character, by scene, or by chapter**

ChatGPT Prompt Examples for Simulated Beta Readers

"Act as a beta reader. Read this chapter and tell me what worked, what didn't, and what confused you."
"Give me feedback from the perspective of a 30-year-old woman reading this romance."
"Read this passage as if you were a young adult fantasy fan. What would excite you? What would bore you?"
"Pretend to be a critical beta reader. What parts would you suggest I improve before publication?"
"Which character stands out most in this chapter, and why?"
"What part of this story did you emotionally connect with, and what felt flat?"
"Act as a children's book reviewer. How age-appropriate and clear is this story?"

Bonus: Simulate Multiple Readers with Unique Perspectives

You can even have ChatGPT give feedback from different types of readers:

- A visual learner
- A sensitivity reader (for cultural or emotional accuracy)
- A critical thinker who prefers logic
- A fast-paced reader who gets bored easily
- A fan of the genre you're writing in

Try this:
"Act as three beta readers with different preferences. Give each reader's feedback separately:

1. A fantasy superfan
2. A romance-only reader
3. A casual reader new to the genre"

Tips for Better Results

- Be specific about your audience
- Provide **context** (e.g., "This is Chapter 3 of a thriller novel")
- Ask for feedback in sections or chapters (don't overload at once)
- Request **emotional reactions**, not just structural critique
- Use this feedback to **polish before real beta readers or editors** step in

What AI Can't Replace

While ChatGPT is great for initial insight, it doesn't fully replace **human beta readers**, who bring:

- Real-world taste and subjectivity
- Unique life experiences
- Genre familiarity and expectations
- Emotional reactions that aren't based on patterns

Still, AI feedback is a valuable *first layer* — one that saves you time and helps you avoid common issues before wider testing.

"The best authors listen to their readers — even the simulated ones."

Formatting Tips (Word vs. Vellum vs. InDesign)

Choosing the Right Tool to Make Your Book Look Professional

Your manuscript may be brilliant, but if the formatting is clunky or unprofessional, it can turn readers away before the first paragraph is finished. Formatting is the bridge between **manuscript and marketplace** — and choosing the right software can make or break the reading experience.

Whether you're self-publishing an eBook, paperback, or hardcover, the right formatting tool depends on your **technical skill level, design goals, and publishing platform.**

Popular Formatting Tools at a Glance

Tool	Best For	Pros	Cons
Microsoft Word	Basic layouts, early drafts, print PDFs	Accessible, easy to use, good for traditional publishers	Limited design control, tricky for complex layouts
Vellum (Mac only)	Indie authors publishing on Amazon, Apple, Kobo, etc.	Elegant templates, easy to use, perfect for eBooks + print	Mac-only, not highly customizable
Adobe InDesign	Professional typesetting, highly designed books	Ultimate control over layout, great for illustrated & complex nonfiction	Expensive, steep learning curve

Tool	Best For	Pros	Cons
Atticus	All-in-one writing + formatting for indie authors	Cloud-based, similar to Vellum but Windows-friendly	Still growing its feature set
Reedsy Book Editor	Free browser-based formatting	Simple and intuitive, clean designs, great for beginners	Fewer style options, limited output flexibility

When to Use Which

Use Word if you…

- Are submitting to a traditional publisher or editor
- Need to track changes or collaborate
- Are writing a simple interior without design elements

Use Vellum if you…

- Are self-publishing fiction or nonfiction
- Want polished output without graphic design skills
- Plan to publish eBooks + print simultaneously

Use InDesign if you…

- Are producing a coffee table book, children's book, or heavily illustrated book
- Need full control over layout, fonts, spacing, and graphics
- Have a designer background (or access to one)

Use BookDesignTemplates.com

Professional Design Without the Designer Price Tag

BookDesignTemplates.com is a user-friendly platform created by Joel Friedlander (a well-known name in indie publishing) to help authors produce beautifully formatted books—without having to learn complicated software like InDesign.

With a wide selection of **professionally designed templates** for **Word and InDesign**, this site is ideal for authors who want their book to look polished and market-ready while still maintaining full creative control.

Highlights:

- Templates for **fiction, nonfiction, workbooks, and more**
- Designed to meet print-on-demand specs (KDP, IngramSpark, etc.)
- Includes **clear instructions** and easy-to-use formatting styles
- Saves time on layout, spacing, fonts, and consistency
- Excellent for both **first-time authors** and publishing professionals

Whether you're self-publishing your debut novel or formatting a complex business book, BookDesignTemplates.com offers a **bridge between DIY and pro design** — without needing a graphic designer or advanced tech skills.

Tip: Once you've chosen your template, you can ask ChatGPT to help customize content flow, edit formatting language, or even adapt sections to match the structure.

Formatting Tips for Any Tool

- **Set your trim size early** (6"x9", 5.5"x8.5", etc.) so your content fits correctly
- Use **styles** (Heading 1, Normal, Quote, etc.) for consistent spacing
- Don't rely on tabs or spacebar for alignment — use paragraph settings
- Choose **readable fonts**: Garamond, Georgia, or Minion Pro for print
- Mind your **margins and gutter** (especially for printed books)
- Keep **chapter titles consistent** in size, placement, and spacing
- For eBooks: avoid page numbers, use clickable TOCs, and keep formatting simple

ChatGPT Can Help With:

"Format this paragraph in a clean, justified layout for a 6x9 print book."
"Give me a clean chapter layout template for Vellum."
"Remind me of the standard print margins for a 300-page book."
"Explain the difference between serif and sans-serif fonts in book design."
"Help me format my table of contents to be clickable in EPUB."

"Formatting is where words meet design — it's not just how your book reads, but how it *feels* in the hands of your reader."

Final Read-Through Prompts

Using AI to Catch What You Missed Before Publishing

A final read-through is your last chance to catch lingering issues — awkward transitions, inconsistent tone, clunky phrasing, or subtle errors that survived multiple rounds of editing.

ChatGPT can act as your **last set of eyes** when you're too close to the manuscript to see clearly. You can use it to review tone, flow, structure, or even simulate the experience of a new reader encountering your book for the first time.

What a Final Read-Through with AI Can Help You Catch:

- Unnecessary repetition or filler
- Sentences that ramble or confuse
- Inconsistencies in tense, tone, or POV
- Missed transitions between sections or chapters
- Final polish for grammar and clarity
- Emotional pacing and impact
- Passive voice or weak verbs
- Overuse of adverbs or clichés

Prompt Examples for Your Final Pass

"Read this chapter like a fresh reader. What stands out as strong, and what feels off?"
"Can you identify any awkward transitions or weak paragraphs in this section?"
"Check this page for repetition, overuse of passive voice, or filler words."
"What's the emotional tone of this ending? Does it match the rest of the chapter?"
"Make this sound smoother while preserving my voice."

"Pretend you're an editor doing a final pass. What would you flag or tweak?"

Best Practices When Using ChatGPT for Final Review

- Provide **clear direction**: "Focus on tone and clarity" or "Only highlight confusing parts"
- Use **smaller chunks**: One chapter or 2–3 pages at a time yields better results
- Clarify your **audience and purpose**: e.g., "This is for a spiritual nonfiction audience"
- Ask for **summary insights**: "Summarize the key ideas in this chapter — do they land?"
- Use "side-by-side" comparison prompts: "Here's my original paragraph. Can you improve it while keeping the tone casual and heartfelt?"

Combine with Other Tools

After using ChatGPT, you might still want to:

- Run the final draft through **Grammarly or ProWritingAid** for micro-edits
- Read it **aloud** (or use text-to-speech) to catch rhythm and pacing issues
- Ask **a trusted beta reader or editor** to do one final human check

"The goal of the final read isn't perfection — it's alignment. Does your message, tone, and style truly reflect what you meant to say?"

CHAPTER 10: Metadata & Marketing Materials

Keywords and BISAC Categories

How to Help Readers Find Your Book — Without a Marketing Budget

No matter how great your book is, readers can't buy what they can't find. **Keywords** and **BISAC categories** are the **invisible tools** that help your book show up in searches, recommendations, and online store filters. These two elements are **crucial for discoverability** — especially on platforms like Amazon, IngramSpark, Barnes & Noble, and Google Books.

ChatGPT can help you brainstorm relevant keyword phrases and choose the most fitting BISAC (Book Industry Standards and Communications) categories, based on your genre, audience, and themes.

What Are Keywords?

Keywords are the search terms people type into online bookstores to find books like yours.

Examples:

- "energy healing for beginners"
- "romantic suspense with female lead"
- "self-help for anxiety"
- "children's bedtime stories with animals"

You're usually allowed **7–10 keywords** (Amazon KDP, for example). These aren't visible to the buyer but are used in algorithms to match books with readers.

ChatGPT Prompt Examples for Keywords

"Suggest 10 long-tail keywords for a book about Reiki and the Five Elements."
"What are readers searching for in spiritual self-help books right now?"
"Generate keyword phrases for a cozy mystery set in a small town."
"Which keywords would match a children's book about kindness and sharing?"
"Based on this book description, what keywords should I add to help it rank?"

What Are BISAC Categories?

BISAC categories classify your book into **industry-standard genres** so retailers, libraries, and distributors know how to catalog it.

You must choose **at least one primary BISAC** when publishing (IngramSpark requires it; Amazon has their own adapted version but uses similar logic). You can often select **2–3 categories**, but only the first one is typically prioritized in classification.

Example BISACs:

- **HEA027000**: Health & Fitness / Healing / Energy
- **SEL031000**: Self-Help / Personal Growth / General
- **FIC027020**: Fiction / Romance / Contemporary
- **JUV039060**: Juvenile Fiction / Social Themes / Emotions & Feelings

ChatGPT Prompt Examples for BISAC Help

"Based on this book summary, which BISAC categories apply?"
"Suggest three BISAC categories for a memoir about addiction recovery."
"What's the best BISAC for a spiritual fantasy novel with angelic characters?"
"Can you find the BISAC for a children's book teaching mindfulness?"
"Compare BISAC options for a book that blends science and spirituality."

Pro Tip: Think Like a Reader

When choosing keywords and categories, ask yourself:

- What would someone type to find *this* book if they didn't know the title?
- What books show up when you search your keywords — are they similar to yours?
- Do the BISAC categories reflect **what the book is really about** — not just where you *want* it to be?

"Keywords are your lighthouse. BISACs are your map. Without both, your book is just drifting in the digital ocean."

SEO-Optimized Descriptions

Crafting Book Descriptions That Attract Readers and Search Engines

Your book description is more than just a summary — it's a **sales tool**. On platforms like Amazon, Google Books, and Kobo, it's also part of your **search engine optimization (SEO)** strategy. The right words can help your book show up in searches, drive clicks, and increase conversions.

A strong, SEO-optimized description should:

- Hook the reader emotionally
- Highlight the value or experience of the book
- Include relevant keyword phrases
- Be formatted for readability (especially online)

ChatGPT can help you craft both long and short-form descriptions that **speak to your audience** and **perform well in search rankings.**

Goals of an SEO Book Description

- **Entice** readers in the first 2–3 lines (especially for Amazon preview)
- **Summarize** the storyline, theme, or benefits clearly
- **Include keywords** naturally (not stuffed or forced)
- **Reflect your genre's tone** — whether emotional, suspenseful, funny, or informative
- **Prompt action** ("Scroll up and buy now," "Start your healing journey today")

SEO Strategies for Book Descriptions

Element	Description
Primary Keywords	Terms readers would search for, like "grief recovery journal" or "fantasy romance with dragons"
Secondary Keywords	Related phrases, e.g., "emotional healing," "epic fantasy adventure"
Calls-to-Action	Phrases like "Grab your copy now," "Perfect for fans of…"
Genre Markers	Include cues like "fast-paced," "heartwarming," "step-by-step guide" to signal content

Prompt Examples for SEO Descriptions

"Write an SEO-optimized book description for a self-help book on manifestation."
"Here's my old book blurb. Can you rewrite it with better flow and keywords?"
"Write a 150-word Amazon-style description for a cozy mystery with a psychic cat."
"Make this sound more compelling and include keywords like 'trauma healing,' 'energy work,' and 'spiritual wellness.'"
"Add a strong first sentence hook to this description."
"Format this into two short paragraphs with bullet points and a CTA at the end."

ChatGPT Can Help You:

- Generate **A/B versions** of your book description to test different tones
- Optimize **different lengths** for Amazon, your website, or email promos
- Create **blurbs with embedded SEO** for both fiction and nonfiction
- Rewrite blurbs for **specific audiences** (young adults, spiritual seekers, coaches, etc.)

Example: Before and After

Before:

This book is about energy healing and chakras. It explains the basics and offers exercises for readers.

After (SEO-Optimized):

Discover the healing power within.

Reiki & the Chakra Journey is your step-by-step guide to restoring energetic balance, reducing emotional stress, and connecting with your higher self. Whether you're new to energy healing or a seasoned practitioner, this empowering book walks you through real-world tools for spiritual growth, chakra alignment, and emotional clarity.

✔ Beginner-friendly techniques
✔ Chakra charts and guided meditations
✔ Practical energy clearing rituals

Ideal for fans of energy medicine, holistic healing, and spiritual wellness.

Start your healing journey today. Scroll up and get your copy now.

"An SEO-optimized description isn't about tricking the algorithm — it's about helping the *right* readers find the book they didn't know they needed."

Social Media Captions & Ads

Using ChatGPT to Create Scroll-Stopping Content that Sells Your Book

Once your book is published, your next challenge is getting it in front of readers — and social media is one of the most powerful tools to do that. But writing daily captions, compelling ads, and call-to-action posts can quickly become overwhelming.

That's where ChatGPT becomes your **content creation assistant**, helping you generate tailored posts for platforms like **Instagram, TikTok, Facebook, Pinterest, X (Twitter), and YouTube Shorts**.

Whether you're writing fiction, nonfiction, or children's books, AI can help you create content that matches your brand tone, hooks attention in seconds, and encourages engagement or sales.

TYPES OF CONTENT CHATGPT CAN HELP YOU CREATE

- **Engaging Captions** (quotes, behind-the-scenes, character teasers)
- **Book Launch Announcements**
- **Story-Based Sales Posts** (use micro-stories to hook readers)
- **Video Hooks** for TikTok or Reels
- **Author Q&A-style Posts**
- **Reader Challenges or Giveaways**
- **Ad Copy** for Meta (Facebook/Instagram) or Amazon Ads
- **Newsletter teasers** that can be repurposed for socials

Prompt Examples for Captions & Ads

"Write 5 Instagram captions to promote a new spiritual healing book, using an empowering tone."
"Create a TikTok script to promote a cozy mystery novel featuring a psychic dog."
"Give me 3 captions that highlight a reader testimonial for my nonfiction productivity book."
"Create a Facebook ad for a children's bedtime book, with emotional appeal to parents."
"Turn this book description into a high-converting short caption with a CTA."
"Write 5 ad variations for a self-help journal launch, each with a different hook (problem, curiosity, transformation, quote, question)."

Copy Structures That Work Well

Format	Example
Hook + Pain + Solution	"Still stuck in self-doubt? This book rewires your mindset in just 5 minutes a day."
Quote + Reaction	"'The energy you give is the energy you receive.' — *Reiki & the Five Elements* 🦋"
Mini-Story	"When Claire lost her job, she never expected a vineyard — and a man with a secret — to change everything..."
Question-Based	"What if your intuition was your most powerful business tool?"
Bold Claim	"This book will help you finish your novel — even if you've failed 10 times before."

Pro Tip: Batch Your Content

Use ChatGPT to plan your **monthly content calendar**:

"Create 15 post ideas to promote my nonfiction book on energy healing, using 3 content pillars: education, story, and engagement."

Then follow up with:

"Now write captions for each of these posts, using a wise but down-to-earth tone."

Sample Captions by Genre

Fiction (Romance):

"Can love bloom in the vineyard's shadow? Escape into *Under the Okanagan Sun* — where the past whispers and the present heals."

Nonfiction (Self-Help):

"Healing doesn't happen in a day, but it starts with a decision. Your energy reset begins here."

Children's Book:

"Bedtime just got magical. *Luna the Light Bearer* helps kids feel safe, seen, and sleepy."

"You don't need to go viral. You just need the right words to reach the right people — and ChatGPT can help you find them."

Book Funnel Suggestions

Turn a Single Book into a Business with ChatGPT's Help

Publishing a book is no longer the end — it's the beginning of your **author journey**. A well-designed **book funnel** transforms readers into subscribers, clients, students, or fans by offering **intentional next steps**.

Think of a funnel as a guided path:
📖 Book → 🎁 Free Gift → 📫 Email Nurture → 💡 Offer → ❤️ Loyalty

ChatGPT can help you craft every stage of that funnel — from creating irresistible lead magnets to writing automated email sequences and even scripting webinar or course invitations.

Book Funnel Flow Overview

Stage	Purpose	What ChatGPT Can Help With
1. Lead Magnet	Attract email subscribers	Free chapter, worksheet, quiz, checklist
2. Landing Page	Convert interest into email opt-in	Headline, benefits, form copy
3. Welcome Sequence	Build trust + connection	3–5 email sequence to introduce your brand
4. Nurture Content	Provide ongoing value	Educational emails, blog ideas, tips, reels

Stage	Purpose	What ChatGPT Can Help With
5. Core Offer	Monetize trust	Course, coaching, journal, bundle, subscription
6. Upsell or Invite	Keep engagement growing	Masterclasses, retreats, VIP services, more books

Prompt Examples for Funnel Creation

"Give me 3 lead magnet ideas based on my energy healing book."
"Write a 5-part welcome email sequence for a new reader who downloaded my chakra checklist."
"Help me write a high-converting headline for my book landing page."
"Create 3 nurture emails with story-based education on manifestation techniques."
"Draft a sales email that introduces my online course connected to this book."
"Suggest a soft upsell at the end of my eBook for readers to join my email list."

Lead Magnet Ideas by Genre

NONFICTION (Wellness, Self-Help):

- "5 Energy Healing Rituals to Balance Your Week"
- "Downloadable Chakra Journal Pages"
- "Quick-Fix Acupressure Chart (PDF)"

FICTION (Romance, Fantasy, Mystery):

- "Bonus Scene You Won't Find in the Book"
- "Map of the World + Character Cheat Sheet"
- "Which Heroine Are You?" Personality Quiz

CHILDREN'S BOOKS:

- "Coloring Pages of the Characters"
- "Printable Affirmation Cards for Kids"
- "Bedtime Routine Checklist (Themed to Book)"

Pro Tip: Make the Funnel Feel Natural

Use prompts like:

"How do I naturally mention my free bonus download in the last page of a novel?"
"Give me subtle call-to-action wording that doesn't feel salesy."
"Write a page 1 teaser that entices readers to opt into my bonus content."

Funnel Success Depends on:

- A **clear, easy-to-understand offer**
- Strong emotional **or practical benefit** to the reader
- Trust built through **tone and value**
- Repetition without feeling like a hard sell
- Using the book's theme or tone to extend the journey

"A book is a doorway. A funnel is the path through it — and ChatGPT can help you build both."

Newsletter and Email Copy

Build Connection, Grow Your List, and Nurture Your Readers with the Help of AI

Newsletters are one of the **most powerful tools** an author can use to build lasting relationships with readers. Whether you're announcing a book launch, sharing behind-the-scenes insights, or offering special bonuses, email allows you to **speak directly to your audience**—without relying on social algorithms.

ChatGPT can help you brainstorm, draft, and polish high-impact email content that maintains your voice while saving you time. From **automated welcome series** to **monthly story-driven updates**, you can create a full strategy that builds trust and gently guides readers to take action.

Email Types ChatGPT Can Help You Write

Email Type	Purpose
Welcome Sequence	Introduce you and your books, build trust, invite engagement
Launch Emails	Create excitement and drive sales during your release window
Storytelling Newsletters	Build a personal bond through themed stories or reader insights
Value Emails	Teach, inspire, or offer tips based on your book's themes
Event Announcements	Let readers know about workshops, signings, or courses

Email Type	Purpose
Sales/Promo Emails	Offer discounts, bundles, or seasonal bonuses
Survey or Feedback Requests	Involve readers and gather insights

Prompt Examples for Newsletter & Email Copy

"Write a 5-part welcome email series for readers of my spiritual wellness book."
"Create a launch sequence with curiosity and storytelling for my new romance novel."
"Turn this blog post into a monthly newsletter update with a call to action."
"Write a re-engagement email for subscribers who haven't opened my last 5 emails."
"Give me 3 email subject line variations that will increase open rates."
"Help me write a value-packed newsletter about intuitive healing techniques from my book."

Email Writing Tips with AI

- **Keep your voice authentic**: Tell ChatGPT, "Use a warm, encouraging tone like my teaching style."
- **Keep it short and skimmable**: Break long sections into smaller paragraphs or bullet points.
- **Use a clear CTA**: Every email should include a next step (read, download, buy, reply).
- **Segment if possible**: ChatGPT can help write different versions for fiction fans vs. nonfiction readers.

Sample Welcome Email (Nonfiction Author)

Subject Line: "Welcome — Your Energy Healing Journey Starts Here"

Body:
Hi [First Name],

I'm so glad you're here. Whether you found me through my book *Reiki & the Five Elements* or through a friend, you've just taken the first step on a powerful path of transformation.

Over the next few emails, I'll be sharing resources, rituals, and personal stories that I don't share anywhere else. If you're ready to align your energy, deepen your healing, and expand your awareness, you're in the right place.

Start here: [Free Chakra Reset PDF]
And if you want to reply and tell me where you are on your healing journey, I'd love to hear from you.

In energy and clarity,
Dr. Constance Santego

"Your book creates the spark. Your emails keep the flame alive."

Prompt Examples:

"Write a 3-Post Launch Sequence…"

AI-Powered Launch Content to Build Buzz and Drive Sales

When launching a new book, having a strong **social media and email sequence** is key to building momentum. ChatGPT can generate customized content that teases your launch, showcases the value of your book, and encourages readers to buy or share.

This section gives you exact **prompt examples** to use when asking ChatGPT to help you create a **3-post (or email) launch sequence** — whether you're promoting a fiction novel, nonfiction guide, children's book, or even a journal or workbook.

Prompt Structure for a 3-Post Launch Sequence

Each post/email in the sequence should follow this rough outline:

1. **Teaser Post (Curiosity & Engagement)**
2. **Announcement Post (Value & Excitement)**
3. **Call to Action Post (Buy Now, Limited Offer, Bonus Gift, etc.)**

Prompt Examples to Use with ChatGPT

GENERAL

"Write a 3-post launch sequence for my upcoming book on using AI as a tool for authors. Make it informative, a bit playful, and conversion-focused."

"I'm launching a children's bedtime book. Write 3 Instagram captions for the week leading up to the launch. Include one with a parent-focused message."

"Write a 3-email sequence to promote my self-help journal. Include a personal story, problem-solution format, and a final email with a discount."

 FOR FICTION

"Create a 3-post launch campaign for my romance novel set in a vineyard. Post 1 = mood teaser, Post 2 = meet the main characters, Post 3 = release day CTA."

"Write 3 Facebook posts for the launch of my fantasy book. Include mystery, worldbuilding teasers, and a limited-time offer."

FOR NONFICTION

"Write a 3-email launch sequence for my nonfiction book about chakra energy healing. Make the first one educational, the second about transformation, and the third a gentle pitch."

"I'm releasing a workbook on intuition. Give me a 3-part sequence to post in my Facebook group, leading to launch day."

FOR CHILDREN'S BOOKS

"Generate 3 short captions for launching a picture book for ages 4–6. Use emotional appeal for parents, and add a tip for bedtime routines in one post."

"Write a launch email sequence for a coloring book with affirmations for kids. Include why it matters and how it helps children feel empowered."

Bonus Tips for Strong Launch Content

- Always include **strong visual prompts**: Ask ChatGPT,

  "Suggest 3 image or video ideas to match each caption."

- Include a **soft or hard CTA**:

  "Preorder now," "Claim your bonus," or "Tag a friend who needs this."

"The key to a great launch isn't shouting the loudest — it's showing up consistently, with clarity and heart."

CHAPTER 11: Publishing & Beyond

Traditional vs. Indie Publishing: How AI Helps Both

No matter your publishing path,
AI is your silent co-author

Whether you dream of landing a traditional publishing deal or prefer the freedom and speed of indie publishing, **AI is a versatile tool that supports every step of the process**. While the paths differ in production, control, and timelines, ChatGPT (and similar tools) can help you stay organized, creative, and productive in either direction.

Let's break down the **key differences** between these two models and how AI can support your success in both.

Traditional Publishing

What It Is:
You submit your manuscript to agents or publishers, who may offer you a contract to publish your book. They handle editing, design, printing, and distribution — often at no upfront cost to you.

Pros:

- Professional editing, cover design, and marketing
- Prestige and bookstore access
- No out-of-pocket expenses to publish

Cons:

- Slower process (12–24 months is common)
- Less creative control
- Smaller royalty share
- Gatekeeping (querying agents is competitive)

How ChatGPT Helps:

- Crafting your **query letter** and **synopsis**
- Polishing your **manuscript before submission**
- Helping you **research agents** or write compelling **book proposals**
- Practicing interview Q&As or **pitch sessions**
- Simulating **beta reader feedback** for early drafts
- Generating **book comps** and genre positioning for proposals

Prompt Example:

"Write a professional query letter for a 75,000-word mystery novel set in a small coastal town."

"List 10 comparable titles to a romantic suspense novel with paranormal elements."

Indie (Self) Publishing

What It Is:
You take on the publishing role yourself or hire freelancers. You retain full rights and royalties while managing production, marketing, and sales.

Pros:

- Full control over creative and business decisions
- Faster time-to-market
- Higher royalty rates
- Direct audience access (email list, website, etc.)

Cons:

- Upfront costs (editing, design, ads)
- Requires business mindset
- You manage or outsource everything

How ChatGPT Helps:

- Generating **titles, blurbs, and chapter summaries**
- Helping structure and **write your book from idea to final draft**
- Creating **marketing copy**, newsletters, and launch plans
- Offering **editing suggestions** and style adjustments
- Writing **social media posts**, **ads**, or even **Amazon SEO descriptions**
- Building out **your author brand voice** over time

Prompt Example:
"Help me write a back cover description for a self-help book on intuitive living."
"Suggest 3 book titles and subtitles that are SEO-friendly for Amazon."
"Write a 5-part email sequence to promote my indie-published memoir."

Hybrid Authors Can Use AI Too

Many authors blend both approaches — traditionally publishing one genre while self-publishing another. AI adapts easily across all workflows.

Use it to:

- Keep your **tone consistent across series**
- Brainstorm content for **your newsletter or blog**
- Prepare **talking points for interviews or book events**

Whichever path you choose, ChatGPT is your behind-the-scenes assistant — helping you write faster, market smarter, and create with clarity.

"Traditional publishing gives you structure. Indie publishing gives you freedom. AI gives you power in both."

Asking ChatGPT About Contracts, Royalties, & Publishing Terms

Understand industry language and protect your rights with AI as your guide

The publishing world is full of complex jargon — from **advance payments** to **royalty splits**, **subsidiary rights**, and **reversion clauses**. If you're a new author (or even a seasoned one), these terms can feel overwhelming.

While ChatGPT is **not a lawyer**, it can help you *understand the basics, translate contract language*, and *prepare intelligent questions* for real professionals. It's like having a publishing dictionary and explainer in your pocket — available 24/7.

What ChatGPT Can Help With:

- Define publishing terms clearly
- Explain royalty structures (traditional vs. self-publishing)
- Offer examples of clauses in layman's terms
- Break down the difference between licensing, rights, and ownership
- Help you compare contract offers or publishing platforms
- Suggest questions to ask a literary agent, publisher, or lawyer

Prompt Example:
"Explain what a 'non-compete clause' means in a publishing contract."
"What does a 10% net royalty on print books actually mean for the author?"
"Give me questions to ask a hybrid publisher before signing a contract."
"What rights should I retain if I self-publish my book?"
"Compare the royalty rates between Amazon KDP, IngramSpark,

and Draft2Digital."

"Translate this contract clause into plain English…" *(paste your clause)*

What ChatGPT Cannot Do:

- Provide legal advice
- Review contracts for legal validity
- Replace a qualified publishing lawyer or literary agent

ChatGPT should be used as a **starting point**, not a substitute, when legal agreements are involved. Think of it as your research buddy — helping you ask smarter questions and feel more confident in professional conversations.

Key Terms to Explore with ChatGPT:

- Advance vs. Royalties
- Net Profit vs. List Price
- Subsidiary Rights (audio, film, translation)
- Work-for-Hire vs. Creator-Owned
- Print-on-Demand Terms
- Reversion of Rights
- Territory & Distribution Limits
- Copyright Ownership
- Exclusivity Clauses

"The more you understand the terms of your book deal, the more empowered you are to protect your voice and your vision."

Self-Publishing Checklists

Everything you need to finish your book, hit publish, and do it professionally—with help from ChatGPT.

Self-publishing gives you **creative freedom** and **total control**, but it also means you're in charge of every step—writing, editing, formatting, publishing, marketing, and beyond. That's where checklists come in. And guess what? ChatGPT can help you **build, customize, and manage** them for every stage of your journey.

Whether you're publishing a novel, nonfiction guide, children's book, or workbook, these structured checklists ensure nothing slips through the cracks.

1. Pre-Publication Checklist

Writing & Editing

- Final draft completed
- Book edited (self or professional)
- Beta reader feedback reviewed
- Revisions made
- Consistency & voice review
- Proofreading pass complete

ChatGPT Prompt:
"Create a pre-publication checklist for a nonfiction book on energy healing."

2. Design & Formatting Checklist

Interior Layout

- Trim size chosen (e.g., 6x9")
- Margins, headers, page numbers set
- Formatting done (Word, Vellum, InDesign, etc.)
- Front and back matter included

Cover Design

- Front cover designed
- Spine and back cover complete
- Blurb finalized
- Print-ready PDF uploaded

ChatGPT Prompt:
"Help me list what's needed for a print-ready book cover using IngramSpark."

3. Platform Setup Checklist

Publishing Platforms

- ISBN purchased or assigned
- KDP/IngramSpark/D2D account set up
- Metadata entered (title, subtitle, keywords, categories)
- Upload files (PDF/ePub)
- Set pricing and territories
- Proof copy ordered and reviewed

ChatGPT Prompt:
"Create a checklist to upload and publish my book on Amazon KDP."

4. Marketing & Launch Checklist

Before Launch

- Author website updated
- Email list ready
- Book funnel or lead magnet created
- Launch team or ARC readers organized
- Press release drafted

During Launch

- 3–5 social posts scheduled
- Newsletter announcement sent
- Discounts or bonuses promoted
- Live reading or event scheduled

After Launch

- Gather early reviews
- Run ads (Amazon/Facebook/Instagram)
- Monitor rankings and sales
- Engage with readers online

ChatGPT Prompt:
"What should I do the week before launching a children's picture book?"

5. Post-Publishing Checklist

- Thank you email to subscribers
- Book added to author platform/store
- Print and ebook versions linked
- Media kit created
- Update Amazon Author Central page
- Plan next promotion or event

Bonus: Ask ChatGPT to Build a Custom Checklist

You can tailor every checklist to your specific genre, format, and timeline.

"Build a checklist for a self-published workbook that includes printing bulk copies and local distribution."
"Create a publishing timeline checklist for a novel I want to launch in 90 days."

"Checklists turn overwhelm into action—and ChatGPT helps you stay on track every step of the way."

How to Write a Press Release or Media Kit

Get media-ready with professional assets crafted by AI.

Whether you're launching your first book or your fifteenth, having a compelling **press release** and a professional **media kit** boosts your visibility and credibility. These tools help bloggers, podcasters, bookstores, reviewers, and journalists easily talk about you and your book — which can lead to more exposure, features, and sales.

With ChatGPT, you don't need to start from scratch. You can generate polished, media-friendly content that's ready to send.

What Is a Press Release?

A **press release** is a short, formal announcement sent to media outlets about your book's launch, award, event, or milestone. It follows a journalistic structure and answers the key questions:

WHO, WHAT, WHEN, WHERE, WHY, AND HOW

What Is a Media Kit?

A **media kit** is a downloadable package (PDF or webpage) that includes:

- Author bio (short + long)
- Book description (short + long)
- High-res author photo
- Book cover image
- Key quotes or reviews
- Interview topics or sample questions
- Contact info & links

Prompt Examples for ChatGPT:

Press Release

"Write a press release for the launch of my new nonfiction book titled *How to Use ChatGPT for Authors*. Target independent author blogs and self-publishing media."

"Generate a short press release for a fantasy novel release, including a hook, book description, and author quote."

Media Kit Assets

"Create a media kit checklist for a debut self-help author."

"Write a 150-word author bio for a natural medicine doctor and multi-genre author."

"Generate 5 interview questions based on my book *Secrets of a Healer* that would appeal to podcast hosts."

"List media outlets, blogs, or podcast types I could reach out to for a book on energy medicine."

Pro Tip: Ask ChatGPT to Adapt Content

"Rewrite this press release in a more casual tone."
"Make my media kit content more compelling for health & wellness audiences."
"List 3 subject lines I can use for pitching this press release to media contacts."

Media Kit Checklist (What to Include)

- Author Bio (Short & Long)
- Book Description (Back Cover Blurb + Extended Summary)
- High-Res Headshot & Cover Image
- Launch Date + Retail Links
- Sample Interview Questions
- Pull Quotes or Reviews
- Contact Information
- Social Media & Website Links

"If your book is the message, your media kit is the megaphone."

Building Your Author Platform with AI Support

Use AI to create, grow, and maintain a powerful author presence.

An **author platform** is more than just a website or social media profile — it's the **total visibility, credibility, and connection you have with your audience**. Whether you're just starting or scaling a career, your platform is what sells books before (and after) they're written.

With ChatGPT as your assistant, you can build that platform strategically, authentically, and efficiently — even if you're not a marketer.

WHAT MAKES AN AUTHOR PLATFORM?

An author platform includes:

- A branded **website**
- **Email list** and newsletter strategy
- **Social media** presence and engagement
- Published books or **samples of your work**
- **Speaking events**, podcasts, media features
- A recognizable **message or theme**

It's the foundation that supports **your book launches, visibility, and career growth**.

How ChatGPT Can Help You Build It:

1. Author Brand Development

- Clarify your niche and audience
- Identify your author tone and message
- Create an elevator pitch or author tagline

Prompt Example:
"Help me create an author tagline if I write holistic wellness nonfiction books."
"What are 3 branding themes for a spiritual fiction author?"

2. Website Copy & Structure

- Write homepage, about, and book pages
- Suggest site structure for authors
- Create SEO-optimized blurbs

Prompt Example:
"Write my About page as an author who blends energy medicine and storytelling."
"Suggest a homepage layout for a fiction author website."

3. Email Strategy

- Write lead magnets, welcome sequences, and newsletters
- Suggest content calendars for weekly/biweekly emails
- Create freebie ideas tied to your books

Prompt Example:
"Write a 3-part welcome email sequence for a reader who downloads my meditation journal."

4. Social Media Presence

- Suggest platforms that fit your personality and genre
- Plan a month of posts (educational, inspirational, personal, promotional)
- Write captions and hashtag suggestions

Prompt Example:
"Plan 5 Instagram post ideas for launching a new fantasy novel."
"Create a content calendar for TikTok if I'm marketing my spiritual memoir."

5. Audience Growth & Connection

- Plan reader polls, giveaways, or book club content
- Generate blog or video content ideas
- Create speaking topics or workshop outlines

Prompt Example:
"List 10 blog topics for an author of children's picture books about emotions."
"Help me outline a 30-minute talk on intuitive writing."

Bonus Tip: Use ChatGPT to Simulate Readers or Followers

If you're unsure what your audience wants, ask ChatGPT to role-play your ideal reader.

"Act as a first-time author website visitor. What would you want to see?"
"Simulate a potential reader and list what questions they might have about my energy healing book."

"Your platform is your lighthouse.
AI helps you keep the light steady
and bright."

CHAPTER 12: AI Etiquette & Responsible Authorship

Building Your Author Platform with AI Support

Use AI to create, grow, and maintain a powerful author presence.

An **author platform** is more than just a website or social media profile — it's the **total visibility, credibility, and connection you have with your audience**. Whether you're just starting or scaling a career, your platform is what sells books before (and after) they're written.

With ChatGPT as your assistant, you can build that platform strategically, authentically, and efficiently — even if you're not a marketer.

WHAT MAKES AN AUTHOR PLATFORM?

An author platform includes:

- A branded **website**
- **Email list** and newsletter strategy
- **Social media** presence and engagement
- Published books or **samples of your work**
- **Speaking events**, podcasts, media features
- A recognizable **message or theme**

It's the foundation that supports **your book launches, visibility, and career growth**.

How ChatGPT Can Help You Build It:

1. Author Brand Development

- Clarify your niche and audience
- Identify your author tone and message
- Create an elevator pitch or author tagline

Prompt Example:
"Help me create an author tagline if I write holistic wellness nonfiction books."
"What are 3 branding themes for a spiritual fiction author?"

2. Website Copy & Structure

- Write homepage, about, and book pages
- Suggest site structure for authors
- Create SEO-optimized blurbs

Prompt Example:
"Write my About page as an author who blends energy medicine and storytelling."
"Suggest a homepage layout for a fiction author website."

3. Email Strategy

- Write lead magnets, welcome sequences, and newsletters
- Suggest content calendars for weekly/biweekly emails
- Create freebie ideas tied to your books

Prompt Example:
"Write a 3-part welcome email sequence for a reader who downloads my meditation journal."

4. Social Media Presence

- Suggest platforms that fit your personality and genre
- Plan a month of posts (educational, inspirational, personal, promotional)
- Write captions and hashtag suggestions

Prompt Example:
"Plan 5 Instagram post ideas for launching a new fantasy novel."
"Create a content calendar for TikTok if I'm marketing my spiritual memoir."

5. Audience Growth & Connection

- Plan reader polls, giveaways, or book club content
- Generate blog or video content ideas
- Create speaking topics or workshop outlines

Prompt Example:
"List 10 blog topics for an author of children's picture books about emotions."
"Help me outline a 30-minute talk on intuitive writing."

Bonus Tip: Use ChatGPT to Simulate Readers or Followers

If you're unsure what your audience wants, ask ChatGPT to role-play your ideal reader.

"Act as a first-time author website visitor. What would you want to see?"
"Simulate a potential reader and list what questions they might have about my energy healing book."

"Your platform is your lighthouse.
AI helps you keep the light steady
and bright."

Using AI Without Losing Your Voice

Stay true to your unique expression while letting AI support your creative flow.

One of the biggest concerns authors have about using AI is this:

"Will it sound like *me*?"

The short answer? **Only if you let it.**
ChatGPT can mimic, support, and even elevate your style — but it should never replace your **authentic voice**, message, or emotional truth.

This section is about maintaining your identity as a writer while still using AI to help you move faster, think deeper, and write better.

Your Voice = Your Values + Style + Rhythm

Your author voice includes:

- The **tone** you use (warm, witty, formal, edgy, lyrical…)
- The **vocabulary** you choose (simple, poetic, technical, metaphorical…)
- Your **pacing and sentence rhythm**
- Your **emotional core and perspective**

AI can help reflect that once you **teach it who you are.**

How to Use AI Without Losing Yourself:

1. Feed It Your Voice First

Prompt:
"Here is a paragraph from my writing. Learn my tone and writing style." *(Paste your sample)*
Then follow up with:
"Now rewrite this new section in my voice."

ChatGPT can absorb your tone and mirror it back — but it needs examples.

2. Co-Create, Don't Co-Depend

Use AI to brainstorm, organize, and refine — but always run content through your own filter:

- Does this feel like me?
- Would I say it this way?
- Does this resonate with my reader?

Prompt:
"This sounds too generic. Rewrite it with more of my unique voice — like the example I gave earlier."

3. Use Prompts That Prioritize Voice

"Write this in a casual, insightful tone like Brené Brown."
"Rewrite with more metaphor, emotional depth, and spiritual nuance."
"Make this sound like a passionate wellness author writing to her tribe."

Be specific. The clearer your vision, the closer AI gets to your truth.

4. Use AI to Clarify, Not Flatten

Sometimes you're too close to your work to edit objectively. ChatGPT can help:

- Spot inconsistencies in tone
- Smooth out awkward transitions
- Offer variations — *but you choose the final cut*

Prompt:
"Give me 3 versions of this paragraph — one emotional, one playful, and one minimalist."

Your Voice Is the Non-Negotiable

Use AI as your assistant — not your ghostwriter. The most powerful books written with ChatGPT are those where the author's **soul still leads the page**.

"AI can learn your voice. But only you can speak your truth."

Avoiding Overdependence

Use ChatGPT as a powerful tool
—not a creative crutch.

As helpful as ChatGPT is, there's a fine line between **support** and **substitution**. The goal of using AI in your writing practice is to **enhance your voice, not erase it** — to speed up your process, not to disconnect from your own creativity.

Many authors worry:

"If I use ChatGPT too much, am I really the one writing my book?"
The answer depends on **how you use it** — not whether you use it at all.

Signs You Might Be Becoming Overdependent

- You copy-paste content without reviewing or rewriting it
- You avoid writing from scratch altogether
- You start feeling disconnected from your message
- Your work sounds generic or inconsistent
- You stop learning, exploring, or evolving your writing craft

AI is meant to be your **creative partner**, not your replacement.

Healthy Ways to Use AI in Moderation

1. Use It for Clarity, Not Creativity

Let ChatGPT help **organize**, **summarize**, or **expand** your ideas — but the core inspiration should still come from **you**.

Prompt:
"Summarize my ideas so I can refine them in my own words."
"List pros and cons of this outline so I can decide what to keep."

2. Alternate Between Solo and Assisted Writing

Try this rhythm:

- **You write the first draft**, then let ChatGPT help revise
- Or **ask ChatGPT to generate options**, then rewrite them in your own tone

Writing first, AI second keeps **your voice** in charge.

3. Practice Writing Without Prompts

If you're always waiting for the perfect prompt, you're not exercising your **creative muscles**. Set a timer. Write freely for 15–30 minutes. Then come back to AI for support or feedback.

4. Reflect On Your Dependency

Ask yourself:

- Am I using this to avoid fear or uncertainty?
- Am I growing or just producing?
- What part of writing still feels magical to me?

ChatGPT is here to serve your growth — not to numb your discomfort.

Reclaiming the Joy of Writing

Writing is messy. It's emotional. It's uniquely human. Don't hand it all over to the machine. Use ChatGPT to **enhance**, not replace, your joy in the process.

"AI can make you faster — but only your soul makes it art."

AI as Co-Creator: A New Model for Writing

Collaboration, not competition — welcome to the age of human-AI storytelling.

The idea of authorship is evolving. Once seen as a solitary endeavor, writing is now entering a new era where **AI doesn't replace the writer — it partners with them**. This isn't the end of creativity; it's the **next chapter.**

Just as artists embraced new tools — from oil paint to Photoshop — today's writers are learning how to **co-create** with ChatGPT and other AI systems to **enhance expression, speed up production**, and **unlock unexpected ideas**.

WHAT IT MEANS TO BE A CO-CREATOR WITH AI

Being a co-creator means:

- You lead the **vision**
- AI contributes **structure, suggestions, and stimulation**
- You **refine, direct, and interpret** the outputs
- The **final voice** is yours — infused with intuition, feeling, and judgment

Think of AI as your:

- **Writing assistant** (organizing and formatting)
- **Creative mirror** (reflecting your tone, testing ideas)
- **Idea generator** (pushing past blocks and expanding your perspective)
- **Collaborator** (building out worlds, characters, data, and prompts you didn't think to ask)

Benefits of Co-Creation with ChatGPT

- **Increased speed:** Outline, draft, and revise faster
- **Deeper development:** Explore characters, subplots, or arguments more thoroughly
- **Greater consistency:** Maintain tone, pacing, and structure throughout
- **More experimentation:** Try styles or genres outside your comfort zone
- **Sustained motivation:** Stay moving when your energy dips

Prompt:
"What are some creative plot twists for this outline?"
"Help me deepen this character's emotional arc."
"Write this argument in a more persuasive tone, with examples."

Co-Creation in Practice

1. **You Define the Vision:** "I'm writing a magical realism novel about healing and generational trauma."
2. **AI Expands Possibilities:** "Generate 10 mystical settings that mirror internal emotional journeys."
3. **You Curate and Shape:** Combine the elements that resonate. Rewrite. Add nuance.
4. **AI Assists in Production:** Format, refine, repurpose (e.g., into blurbs, summaries, newsletters)

Balance: Technology + Intuition

This new model isn't about outsourcing creativity. It's about creating a **synergy between the logical and the intuitive,** the fast and the thoughtful, the structured and the soul-led.

You bring the **meaning**.
AI brings the **momentum**.

"The future of writing isn't man or machine — it's man with machine. Together, we become something more."

The Future of AI in Writing

From tool to teammate — AI is transforming the literary landscape.

We are witnessing a profound shift in the creative world. Artificial intelligence, once seen as a novelty or threat, is evolving into something far more impactful: **a collaborative force shaping the future of storytelling**.

As the technology becomes more refined and intuitive, the way we write, publish, and even define "authorship" is expanding. AI is not replacing writers — it's **redefining the process** by making it more accessible, faster, and in some cases, more imaginative.

What's Emerging Now

1. Frictionless Creation

Writers no longer have to fear the blank page. With AI, you can:

- Start faster with instant outlines or summaries
- Keep momentum when you're stuck
- Rework chapters or scenes without waiting for critique partners

This means **fewer abandoned manuscripts** and **more finished books**.

2. Multimedia Storytelling

AI is no longer limited to just words. You can now:

- **Generate illustrations** for children's books
- **Convert written scenes into audio narration**
- **Turn characters into animated avatars**
- **Build interactive fiction or choose-your-path adventures**

The future writer may not just be an author — but a **creator-director** of immersive storytelling experiences.

3. Real-Time Audience Interaction

With AI and tools like chatbots or character simulations, authors can:

- Let readers **talk to their characters**
- Create AI-enhanced **book club guides**
- Deliver **dynamic bonus content** or alternate endings
- Simulate Q&As, fan fiction ideas, or worldbuilding expansion

The line between **reader and writer is blurring** — and that's opening doors to deeper engagement.

4. New Publishing Models

Imagine:

- AI-powered **editors and layout assistants**
- Entire book series developed through collaborative sprints
- Instant formatting and SEO optimization built into writing tools
- Voice-enabled **dictation and revision systems**

Self-publishing becomes not just viable, but **streamlined**.

5. Creative Ethics & Ownership

As AI continues to evolve, so will questions about:

- **Copyright**: Who owns AI-assisted content?
- **Originality**: What counts as "your work"?
- **Authenticity**: Will readers value books written *with* AI differently than books written *by* humans alone?

Writers who use AI thoughtfully — **transparently and ethically** — will be leaders in defining this next chapter.

Writers of the Future

The author of the future:

- **Co-creates with AI** while honoring their voice
- **Builds books like ecosystems**, not just stories
- **Grows global reach** through automated translation and localization
- **Uses technology to amplify**, not diminish, their soul's message

Whether you're a novelist, children's author, or wellness educator, the tools now available **expand your impact** far beyond the page.

"AI won't replace authors — but authors who embrace AI will shape the next wave of literature."

BONUS SECTION: 100+ Author Prompts

Organized by Phase: Idea, Drafting, Editing, Publishing

"Sometimes, the most powerful prompt is simply: *What should I be asking you?*"

IDEA PHASE PROMPTS

For when you're staring at the blank page or unsure what to write next.

These prompts will help you generate book ideas, explore different genres, define your audience, and clarify your book's core purpose before you write a single word.

Book Concept & Brainstorming

- "Give me 10 unique book ideas for [fiction/nonfiction/memoir/children's] that haven't been done before."
- "Brainstorm book ideas that combine [topic 1] with [topic 2]."
- "What's a powerful metaphor I can build a book around?"
- "Suggest 5 book titles based on this idea: [your idea]."

- "What's a creative angle I can take on [common theme or topic]?"
- "List 10 ways to stand out in the [your niche] category."

Audience Clarity

- "Who is the ideal reader for a book about [topic]?"
- "What are this audience's biggest problems, desires, or questions?"
- "How would I describe this book in one sentence to a [specific audience]?"
- "What tone, style, and format would best suit a book for [audience]?"

Market Research & Trends

- "What are the top-selling books in the [genre/topic] niche this year?"
- "List 5 trends in the [your topic] category I could tap into."
- "What are gaps in the market for books about [topic]?"
- "Compare 3 successful books on [topic] and suggest how mine could be different."

Hooks, Titles & Loglines

- "Write a compelling book hook for a story about [plot or topic]."
- "Suggest 10 working titles for a [genre/topic] book."
- "Turn this idea into a 1-sentence elevator pitch."
- "What would be a compelling subtitle for this title: [Title]?"

Structure Exploration

- "What structure would work best for a book about [topic]?"

- "Give me 3 ways to structure a [fictional story/memoir/self-help guide]."
- "How could I turn this idea into a 5-part or 12-chapter book?"

Genre-Specific Prompts

- "Give me 3 children's book ideas for ages [age range] focused on [theme]."
- "What would be a unique take on a romance/mystery/fantasy/health book?"
- "Help me brainstorm a nonfiction book idea that blends storytelling with education."
- "Create a memoir theme based on these three events in my life: [list events]."

DRAFTING PHASE PROMPTS

Turn your ideas into structured chapters, vibrant scenes, and polished paragraphs.

Use these prompts to develop your outline, deepen your writing, and get unstuck during the creative process. Whether you're writing fiction or nonfiction, these will guide you through generating high-quality content with flow and clarity.

Outlining Your Book

- "Create a detailed chapter outline for a book about [topic/plot]."
- "Break down this outline into 12 chapters: [insert rough idea]."
- "What should I include in each chapter of a book about [topic]?"
- "Suggest a three-act structure for this fiction plot: [insert idea]."

Chapter-Level Support

- "What are the key points I should cover in Chapter 3 about [subject]?"
- "Summarize Chapter 1 of my book idea on [topic] in a compelling way."
- "What's a good transition from Chapter 2 to Chapter 3?"
- "Turn this bullet list into a well-written chapter: [paste bullets]."

Voice & Tone

- "Rewrite this paragraph in a more conversational tone."
- "Adjust the tone to sound more professional/compassionate/inspirational."
- "Make this sound like a thought leader in the wellness space."
- "Rewrite this in a poetic, lyrical style."

Writing Dialogue (Fiction)

- "Create a dialogue between two characters in conflict over [insert issue]."
- "Write a conversation that shows [character] is hiding something."
- "Make this dialogue sound more natural and emotionally layered."

Inner Monologue & Emotion

- "Write a paragraph that shows this character is experiencing grief but trying to hide it."
- "What might [character] be thinking in this moment of betrayal?"
- "Turn this emotional beat into a full scene."

Descriptions & Settings

- "Describe a cozy mountain cabin with magical elements."
- "Make this description more sensory and immersive: [paste text]."
- "Help me write a setting that reflects my character's mood."

Nonfiction Examples & Clarity

- "Give me an example story to illustrate this concept: [insert concept]."
- "List statistics or facts to support a chapter on [topic]."
- "Turn this concept into a relatable analogy or metaphor."

Transitional Sentences & Flow

- "What's a smooth transition from this paragraph to the next?"
- "Write a strong closing paragraph for this chapter."
- "How can I connect these two ideas without losing the reader?"

Writer's Block Busters

- "I'm stuck. Ask me 5 questions that could help me move forward."
- "Give me three alternate ways to express this idea."
- "What happens next in this scene: [describe scene]?"

EDITING PHASE PROMPTS

Shape your raw draft into a compelling, professional-quality manuscript.

These prompts help you fine-tune your work—strengthen your narrative, clarify your message, tighten structure, and preserve your unique voice. Whether you're self-editing or preparing for a professional editor, these will elevate your manuscript with AI's support.

Rewriting for Clarity or Style

- "Rewrite this paragraph to be more clear and concise."
- "Make this more emotional and impactful."
- "Rewrite in a more poetic/literary/comedic tone."
- "Simplify this technical explanation for a general audience."
- "Change this passive voice to active."

Spotting Repetition or Wordiness

- "Highlight and remove repetitive phrases in this passage."
- "Eliminate unnecessary filler words from this text."
- "Rewrite this paragraph without using the word 'that.'"
- "Trim this section by 30% without losing meaning."

Improving Argument or Flow (Nonfiction)

- "Make this argument more persuasive with facts or analogies."
- "Help me create a stronger bridge between these two points."
- "Clarify my central message in this chapter."
- "What's missing in this explanation of [topic]?"

Dialogue Tweaks (Fiction)

- "Make this dialogue sound more natural for a teenager/adult/elder."
- "Tighten this conversation and add subtext."
- "What emotion is missing in this dialogue exchange?"
- "Rewrite this so that each character's voice feels unique."

Structure & Consistency

- "Point out inconsistencies in tone or logic in this chapter."
- "Does the pacing feel rushed or slow in this section?"
- "Create a checklist to ensure POV consistency in my manuscript."
- "Help me reorder these paragraphs for better flow."

Grammar, Punctuation, and Proofreading

- "Find grammar mistakes in this passage."
- "Fix punctuation in this paragraph."
- "Is this sentence grammatically correct: [paste sentence]?"
- "Check this for spelling inconsistencies and suggest improvements."

Polishing Sentences

- "Improve sentence variation in this paragraph."
- "Make this section more lyrical without changing the meaning."
- "Turn these short choppy sentences into smoother ones."
- "What's a more elegant way to say this: [paste sentence]?"

Line-by-Line Feedback

- "Give me feedback on the tone, voice, and clarity of this page."
- "Is this chapter opener strong enough to hook the reader?"

- "Mark any awkward phrasing and suggest smoother alternatives."
- "Is the emotional arc complete in this scene?"

PUBLISHING PHASE PROMPTS

Finish strong with professional presentation, discoverability, and promotional momentum.

These prompts help you get your book ready for release — from final details like titles and keywords to launch content, platform growth, and outreach.

Titles, Subtitles & Back Cover Copy

- "Give me 10 creative title ideas for a book about [topic/storyline]."
- "Suggest a subtitle that makes this book more marketable: [title]."
- "Write a compelling short description for the back cover of this book."
- "Create a longer back cover blurb that captures the emotional journey."
- "Give me 5 hooks I could use for this book's Amazon listing."

Keywords & Categories

- "List keywords to help this book rank on Amazon under [genre/topic]."
- "Suggest the best BISAC categories for a book about [topic]."
- "Create an SEO-optimized product description for a nonfiction book on [topic]."
- "What search terms might my audience use to find this book?"

Marketing & Launch

- "Write a 3-email launch sequence for my new book."
- "Write a social media post to announce my book release with a call to action."
- "Give me 5 caption ideas for Instagram to promote this book."
- "Create a Facebook ad copy targeting [audience] for [book title]."
- "Help me outline a 5-day book launch plan."

Platform Building & Assets

- "Draft a one-page press release announcing this book."
- "Create a media kit with author bio, book summary, and talking points."
- "Write a blog post announcing the book and inviting early reviews."
- "Generate 3 podcast pitch emails based on the book's theme."
- "Suggest newsletter content to promote the book post-launch."

Publishing Options & Guidance

- "What are the pros and cons of self-publishing this book vs. traditional?"
- "Explain the difference between KDP, IngramSpark, and hybrid publishing."
- "What royalty rates can I expect with self-publishing?"
- "Give me a checklist for uploading this book to Amazon KDP."
- "What legal disclosures or copyright steps should I take?"

Post-Launch Support

- "Suggest 10 ways to keep my book visible after launch."
- "How can I turn this book into a course, workshop, or community offering?"
- "Create a reader discussion guide for this book."
- "What bonus content could I offer readers to increase engagement?"
- "Generate a 'thank you for reading' message to include at the end of the book."

Genre-Specific Prompts

Tailor your writing process to your book's unique style, structure, and audience.

Different genres require different voices, conventions, and creative strategies. Whether you're writing a novel, a memoir, a self-help guide, or a children's book, ChatGPT can help you think like a genre expert—even if it's your first time. Use these curated prompts to align with expectations, enhance creativity, and deepen your storytelling or content delivery.

Fiction (General)

- "Give me a story idea that follows the hero's journey in a fantasy setting."
- "List 5 internal and external conflicts for a thriller protagonist."
- "Describe a setting for a dystopian novel that reflects societal decay."
- "What are some lesser-used themes in contemporary romance?"
- "Generate a twist ending for a murder mystery."

Romance

- "Create a meet-cute between a florist and a firefighter."
- "List 3 emotional beats in a slow-burn romance."
- "Give me dialogue that shows unresolved romantic tension."
- "Suggest romantic tropes that work well with enemies-to-lovers."
- "Describe a romantic setting for a second-chance love story."

Fantasy / Sci-Fi

- "Design a unique magical system that's rooted in elemental energy."
- "Describe a futuristic society with 3 major ethical dilemmas."
- "Invent a mythical creature native to a desert planet."
- "What are some lesser-used fantasy quest archetypes?"
- "Give me names for a steampunk airship crew."

Mystery / Thriller / Suspense

- "Outline a locked-room mystery involving a family secret."
- "What clues could foreshadow a betrayal without giving it away?"
- "Describe a detective with an unusual skill or quirk."
- "Generate red herrings for a whodunit plot."
- "Write a high-stakes interrogation scene."

Nonfiction

- "Break down this concept for a beginner audience: [insert topic]."
- "Create a 5-step framework to help readers overcome [problem]."
- "What's a compelling story to illustrate [core idea]?"
- "Write a case study for a chapter on [topic]."
- "Turn this expert-level content into an easy-to-follow chapter."

Children's Books

- "Generate 3 story ideas for ages 4–6 that teach kindness."
- "Suggest a moral lesson suitable for ages 8–10."
- "Write a rhyming couplet about a lost puppy."
- "Describe a magical world that a 7-year-old could imagine."
- "List illustration ideas for a book about overcoming fear."

Memoir / Autobiography

- "Help me outline my personal story around this theme: [e.g., resilience]."
- "What memoir structures could I use if I don't want to go chronologically?"
- "How can I reflect on a traumatic event with compassion and clarity?"
- "Give me 5 questions to reflect on my biggest turning point."
- "Write a scene that captures the emotional truth of this memory: [describe]."

Self-Help / Personal Development

- "Suggest exercises for readers to apply the lesson in this chapter."
- "Create a journaling prompt for someone working on [topic]."
- "Write a motivational paragraph to begin a chapter about confidence."
- "What metaphors can help explain imposter syndrome?"
- "Turn this idea into a 'daily practice' section: [insert idea]."

Productivity: Writing Faster, Smarter, and with Less Burnout

Use ChatGPT as your behind-the-scenes co-writer to get more done in less time—without sacrificing quality.

Writing a book can feel overwhelming. But when used intentionally, AI can streamline your process, reduce decision fatigue, and help you stay focused. Whether you're dealing with procrastination, information overload, or just too many tabs open, these productivity strategies and prompts will keep you moving forward.

Mindset & Momentum Prompts

- "Help me plan a 7-day writing sprint for my book."
- "Give me a motivational message to start today's writing session."
- "Ask me 3 questions to unlock creative flow when I'm stuck."
- "What's the smallest next step I can take right now on my book?"
- "How can I reframe writer's block and keep going?"

Planning & Focus Tools

- "Create a weekly writing schedule based on 1 hour a day."
- "Break this book project into 10 manageable milestones."
- "What tasks should I prioritize this week to keep momentum?"
- "Summarize this chapter's purpose so I stay focused."
- "Outline my next writing session so I know what to tackle."

Efficiency with Prompts

- "Rewrite this section in less than 200 words."
- "Summarize this idea as if explaining it in a Tweet."
- "Create a checklist from this paragraph."
- "Write 5 variations of this sentence so I can choose the best."
- "Turn this messy paragraph into a clear first draft."

Staying Accountable

- "Create a 30-day challenge calendar for finishing my book."
- "Ask me at the end of every session: what did I accomplish?"
- "Help me log my daily writing word count with a short reflection."
- "What rewards can I set for each writing milestone?"
- "How do I create a distraction-free writing ritual?"

Automation & Templates

- "Can you store and recall my style guide for this book?"
- "Give me a reusable prompt template for writing social media captions."
- "Create a standard chapter template I can use throughout this book."
- "Help me batch-create 5 intros/outros in one sitting."
- "What are the repetitive tasks ChatGPT can help me automate?"

With the right AI-powered habits, productivity becomes less about pushing harder—and more about writing smarter.

Block-Busting Prompts: Break Through Writer's Block with AI Support

When the words won't come, ChatGPT can help clear the path.

Writer's block shows up in many forms—overwhelm, indecision, self-doubt, perfectionism, or simply not knowing where to start. This section offers targeted prompts to get unstuck fast, whether you're blocked at the beginning, in the middle, or nearing the finish line.

When You Don't Know What to Say

- "What's one way to start this chapter with curiosity or tension?"
- "Ask me 5 questions that could unlock this scene/topic."
- "Suggest a metaphor or visual to explain this idea clearly."
- "Give me 3 ways to reword this confusing paragraph."
- "What's the easiest part I could write right now to build momentum?"

When You're Second-Guessing Everything

- "What would a confident version of me write here?"
- "Turn this paragraph into a messy first draft—I'll clean it later."
- "Remind me why my message is worth sharing."
- "How can I rewrite this with less pressure and more play?"
- "What would I say if I knew I couldn't fail?"

When You're Overwhelmed or Burned Out

- "Break this big task into 3 simple steps I can do today."
- "Suggest a 15-minute writing task that feels light and fun."
- "What's one sentence I can write to feel like I've made progress?"
- "Help me focus by summarizing what I've already done."
- "Give me a gentle writing prompt to reconnect with joy."

When You Feel Stuck in the Middle

- "What twist or turning point could energize this chapter?"
- "Suggest a bridge paragraph between this section and the next."
- "What's missing that could bring depth or tension here?"
- "Give me 3 emotional beats to move this scene forward."
- "What would surprise or delight my reader right now?"

Quick Reframes & Pattern Breakers

- "Write this as a poem / joke / fairytale to get me out of my head."
- "Use a completely different tone to rewrite this—funny, poetic, sarcastic?"
- "Flip the perspective—what would the antagonist / client / child say here?"
- "What's the opposite of this idea? Explore that for contrast."
- "Give me a completely unexpected way to express this concept."

These prompts are your "creative CPR"—they don't need to be perfect, just enough to get your flow going again.

Tip: If you don't know what prompt to use, try this one: "I feel stuck—what should I ask you next?"

Bibliography

Books & Guides

- Clark, Joanna. *The Writer's Guide to Self-Publishing*. Indie Ink Press, 2020.
- Clark, Joanna. *The Creative Writer's Productivity Manual*. Indie Ink Press, 2021.
- Friedlander, Joel. *A Self-Publisher's Companion: Expert Advice for Authors Who Want to Publish*. Marin Bookworks, 2011.
- Hay, Louise. *You Can Create an Exceptional Life*. Hay House, 2011.
- Kern, Mary. *Digital Writing for the Modern Author*. Pen & Pixel Publishing, 2022.
- Truant, Johnny, and Sean Platt. *Write. Publish. Repeat.* Realm & Sands, 2013.
- Young, Orna. *The Creative Self-Publishing Handbook*. ALLi Publishing, 2020.

AI & Technology

- OpenAI. *ChatGPT: User Documentation and Terms of Use*. Retrieved from https://openai.com
- Roose, Kevin. *Futureproof: 9 Rules for Humans in the Age of Automation*. Random House, 2021.
- Smith, Cal. *The AI Author's Playbook*. Smart Author Press, 2023.
- Tegmark, Max. *Life 3.0: Being Human in the Age of Artificial Intelligence*. Vintage, 2018.

Publishing & Marketing Tools

- Amazon Kindle Direct Publishing. *KDP Help & Resources*. Retrieved from https://kdp.amazon.com
- Reedsy. *Reedsy Publishing Blog & Guides*. Retrieved from https://blog.reedsy.com
- IngramSpark. *Self-Publishing Guide*. Retrieved from https://www.ingramspark.com
- BookDesignTemplates.com. *Author Templates and Design Resources*. Retrieved from https://bookdesigntemplates.com

Style & Editing Tools

- Grammarly. *Grammarly Writing Handbook*. Retrieved from https://grammarly.com
- ProWritingAid. *Editing Tools for Writers*. Retrieved from https://prowritingaid.com
- The Chicago Manual of Style. *17th Edition*. University of Chicago Press, 2017.
- Strunk Jr., William, and E. B. White. *The Elements of Style*. Pearson, 1999.

Blogs & Expert Contributions

- Porterfield, Amy. *Digital Course Academy*. https://www.amyporterfield.com
- Bacher, Caitlin. *Scale with Success Blog*. https://caitlinbacher.com
- Santego, Constance. *Publishing Resources*. https://maximilliane.com/

Message From The Author

Dear Writer,

If you're holding this book, then something inside you is whispering—or maybe shouting—that it's time to create. Whether you're drafting your very first manuscript or already have a bookshelf with your name on it, one thing is certain: the way we write is changing.

When I first explored ChatGPT, I approached it with curiosity and just a touch of skepticism. Could a machine really support the deeply human process of storytelling? What I discovered was something surprising—not a replacement for the writer, but a tool that helps *reveal* the writer within.

This book isn't about shortcuts. It's about support. It's about using AI to **streamline the technical**, **spark the creative**, and **keep you moving** when resistance shows up. It's a co-creative process—one where your voice leads and the AI follows.

As an author, teacher, and lifelong student of personal transformation, I wrote this guide because I believe that *everyone has a book inside them*. And now, with the right guidance and tools, there's no reason to keep it locked away.

So let's write boldly. Let's prompt with purpose. Let's make technology serve your message—not the other way around.

See you on the page.

With creativity and clarity,
Dr. Constance Santego

About The Author

Dr. Constance Santego is a multi-published author, course creator, educator, and visionary in both the holistic wellness and publishing industries. With over 25 years of experience as a Doctor of Natural Medicine and the founder of multiple educational institutions—including 24Karat Beauty Academy and BookWizard Hub—she has guided thousands of students, clients, and authors toward transformation, healing, and creative empowerment.

Her writing spans both fiction and nonfiction, often bridging the worlds of energy medicine, intuitive development, entrepreneurship, and spiritual growth. As a publisher, she has developed dozens of certification programs and has mentored new writers through every stage of authorship—from concept to creation to launch.

Dr. Santego's passion lies in demystifying complex ideas and making them practical and accessible. In *How to Use ChatGPT for Authors*, she blends her expertise in writing and education with emerging AI tools, giving authors a clear, ethical, and empowering path to co-creating their books with confidence.

She currently resides in Kelowna, B.C., where she continues to write, teach, mentor, and inspire others to share their stories—and their truth—with the world.

Website: www.constancesantego.ca
YouTube: @ConstanceSantego
Publisher: Maximillian Enterprises

ALSO AVAILABLE

Play the game *Ikona* – Discover Your Inner Genie

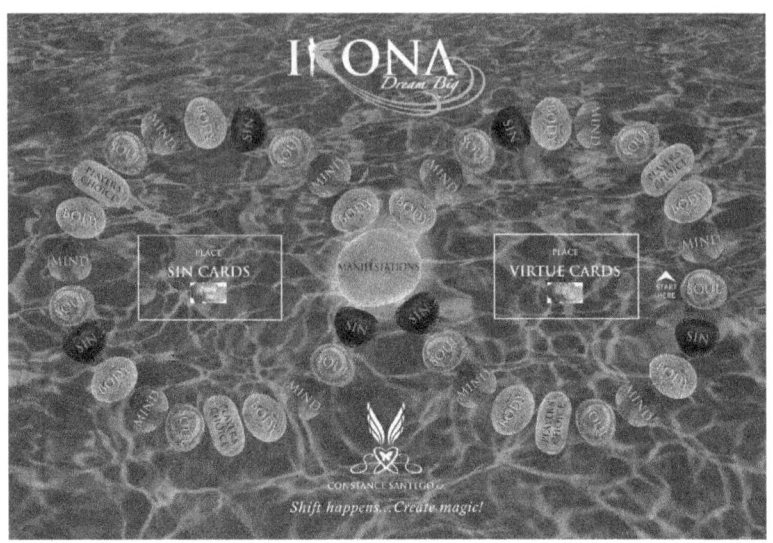

For additional information on

Constance Santego's

wide range of Motivational Products, Coaching Sessions, Spiritual Retreats,
Live Events and Educational Programs

Go to

www.ConstanceSantego.ca

Follow on Instagram - Constance_Santego and
Facebook - constancesantegoo

Subscribe and receive Free Information and Meditations on my
YouTube Channel - Constance Santego

www.ingramcontent.com/pod-product-compliance
Lightning Source LLC
Chambersburg PA
CBHW070906120626
46546CB00001B/158